It's In
YOUR NAME

It's In
YOUR NAME

The exposure of hidden secrets
Unveiling the Sacred Code
The only formula to accurately analyze first names

Garrett Sinclaire

Infinity-Link Publishing
1517 North Wilmot PMB 134
Tucson, Arizona 85712

www.itsinyourname.com

520-298-7391
425-920-7687 fax

Infinity-Link Publishing
1517 North Wilmot PMB 134
Tucson, Arizona 85712
520-298-7391
425-920-7687 fax

www.itsinyourname.com

ISBN 0-9660539-0-7

Printed in the United States of America

Contents

Disclaimer

This book is designed to provide information regarding the subject matter covered. It is sold with the understanding that the author is not engaged in rendering legal, psychological, marital, or other professional services. If expert assistance is required, it should be sought from a competent professional.

It is not the purpose of this book to reprint all the information that is otherwise available to the author, but to complement other texts. It is suggested that you read all the available material, learn as much as possible about the Universal Principles of Life, and tailor the information to your individual needs.

The purpose of this book is to educate and entertain. The author shall have neither responsibility nor liability to any person or entity with respect to any loss or damage alleged to be caused directly or indirectly by the information contained in this book.

About the Author

Garrett Sinclaire was born in Hamburg and raised in Bremen, Germany. On his quest to find his purpose in life and the answers to the discord and misery on this planet, coupled with his understanding that control must come from a higher source, he stumbled over the Sacred Code.

Garrett slowly realized that because of the vastness of this divine knowledge, his work would not be done during his lifetime. So he decided to set in print excerpts, and in 1970 he introduced a curriculum of 1206 lessons divided into 14 subjects that comprise the foundation of the Sacred Wisdom. He continued in the late 1980s with private consultations, lectures and seminars in Los Angeles, California.

Finally, he made available various types of name and compatibility analyses, personal and business forecasts, and he appears as a guest speaker on radio talk shows. Today he is compiling his life's work into several volumes of books, the contents often controversial and, until now, unavailable to the public.

This is the first in a nine-volume series. Introductions to the entire Sacred Code series of books are available at **www.itsinyourname.com**.

Acknowledgements

First and foremost, I would like to present my best wishes to my dear friend and partner in marriage, who was and is adjusting her life to accommodate my need for a peaceful environment and who is enabling me to complete several of my works. Thank you, Jenica, for your time, special efforts, and for your always obliging disposition, as well as your loving care and the personal sacrifices you have endured. I want you to know it will not be forgotten. You reap as you have sown.

My thanks to a number of authorities—federal government departments, libraries, some industrial institutions, ministries, religious non-profit organizations, and periodicals-and the many individuals connected to those organizations who contributed directly or indirectly to the preparation of this book.

A sincerest thanks to: Summer Doucet, Book Partners (**www.bookpartners.net**), Dan Poynter, Para Publishing (**www.danpoynter.com**), and Z. M. Wagner, who supplied me with a wealth of useful information which helped me to succeed in publishing *It's In Your Name*. A special thanks to Mollie Savage, who helped to edit, balance and adjust the chapters and text to make the reading of this book an enjoyable experience (**www.molliesavage.com**).

A number of people contributed directly to the development of *It's In Your Name*. Special thanks go to: Lynette Hill, Carter McBride, Sue Garipoglu, Arif Dogan, Dolores Brown, John Chubb, Ilona Bodi, Charly Sparks, Pauline Malone Hassett, Gary V. Travis, Berta Michaels, Layne G. Kardener, Norma Terril, Gay Abarbanell, Evolene Hawkins, Wilma Ziegler, Bob Davies, Chris Robinson, Madilene Garcia, Elisabeth Morentin, Laura Ferris, Dave Olsen, Caren Halenbeck, Kara Hollenbeck, Paula McHoe, Garaldine Reheis, Jack Danon, Barbara Lodi, Anita Flowers, James Aramant, Gordon Fox, Jenevelan and Michael Stuart.

A few fine people contributed indirectly to this special event. In alphabetical order, special mention goes to: Walter Bauer, Rick Bishop, Ken Fisher, Danny Jenke, Bob Newell, Shorty Reim, Mikal D. Rusnov and Roy Vorce.

Whale picture by:
Rick Bishop, Wild Life Photographer
richard@itsinyourname.com

———————

Foreword

Photograph by Richard Bishop

The average person is not aware of the vast and complex system of the cosmos and the absolute balance it contains, or that his or her existence would never cause a ripple on the sea of life. That we do not understand all life evolved from the sea and do not recognize the mental and spiritual power within ourselves is part of the great plan of life that includes everyone and everything.

Life is a vast sea of time and space. But time and space are little compared to the power of consciousness. The conscious mind is the key to wisdom, the passage of intelligence, and the place where thought is manifested. Life is made conscious through vibration, thus realizing creation.

The Holy Manuscripts discovered together form the Sacred Wisdom. Long ago the Israelites were aware of the power contained in the Holy Manuscripts. First written in Hebrew, the Holy Manuscripts were later translated into many languages and displayed in every country in the world (Colossians 1:26).

The Holy Manuscripts, an expression of the cosmic truth, had no beginning; they always were. "I have been established from everlasting to the beginning, before there was ever an earth" (Proverbs 8:23). Through the Qabbalistic method, "I" symbolizes the Sacred Wisdom.

The Holy Manuscripts were received by Abraham to serve as a guide to physical life on Earth (Genesis 17:7). Later, they would become known to Moses through his apostles and prophets (John 1:17). The Sacred Code, the interconnected three-fold relationship and the workings of the Holy Manuscripts, is the key to opening and understanding the Holy Scriptures.

After Moses handed the Holy Manuscripts to the Israelites, a small number of people took it upon themselves to remove the mechanics from them (Rev.5:1, 3-4). Closely guarded and kept secret for centuries, the Holy Manuscripts in their complete form were available only to a few chosen people in the priesthood (Colossians 1:26).

Since the removal of the Sacred Code from the Holy Manuscripts, people have consistently misinterpreted the contents of the Bible and other sacred documents, so that they have become, at best, contradictory and confusing. The Sacred Code is revealed through the Qabbalistic method, unraveling the mysteries of life (Ephesians 3:3-5).

The Sacred Code contains the Universal Principles of Life, the heart of the Sacred Wisdom. The knowledge existing in the Akashic Records of the spiritual ether of space, it is the memory of the sacred universal intelligence. We see proof of the Sacred Wisdom in the ancient writings of Egypt and South America, of Assyria, Babylon, and in the sacred writings of the Persians. Discovered in Peru, Japan, Asia, Africa, Europe, Australia, and all parts of America, the Sacred Wisdom is inscribed in tables and documented on parchment all over the world in languages as ancient as Greek, Chinese, Latin, and the Sanskrit.

The Kogi Indians of Colombia, South America still live by the ancient wisdom. The Kogi picture the universe in the shape of an enormous egg made of nine layers. The "Mama," or High Priest, the dominant religious and political authority in the Kogi community, acquires his status by undergoing an apprenticeship beginning in his late childhood and lasting nine years. After death, Kogi members are led through the symbolic nine months of gestation until reaching "rebirth" in the next world. (Reincarnation is an integral part of their beliefs.) Similarly, the number nine symbolizes the infinite nature of the universe. The nine layers of the Kogi describe the universe as it is written in ancient manuscripts.

The members of the Kogi tribe see themselves as the guardians of mankind, responsible for maintaining the order and balance of the universe, and Kogi rituals are held to maintain the proper order of the natural world. Birth, initiation and death are the key events in their "life cycle," referred to as the "Cyclic Law" in the Qabbalah. The Cyclic Law is one of the three Universal Principles of Life.

The bestowing of a name is one of the most important events in a Kogi's life; indeed, in Kogi culture, a person is not considered complete until named. The Kogi believe that the right name will enhance the innermost desires through proper expression, something that is well documented throughout the Holy Scriptures.

The Kogi believe they alone are responsible for the orderly succession of the seasons, the coming of the rains at the right time, and even the rising of the sun in the morning and its setting in the evening. The Holy Scriptures, and the practical Qabbala, also reveal how important it is to begin endeavors at the right time. As deeply religious people, the Kogi's beliefs are closely related to their concept of the order and functioning of the universe; the individual and society at large carry the burden of great responsibility. If everyone in the world carried out this belief we would not have the chaos and confusion that exists on Earth today.

According to the Kogi, a man carries within himself a vital polarity of good and evil. The main problem of human existence is to find a harmonic balance between these two

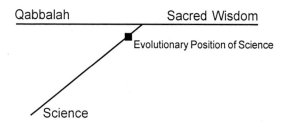

**Crossroads to Wisdom
in the year 2000**

Science offers a universal understanding of all physical matters. The Qabbala offers a universal understanding of the Sacred Wisdom. If this Sacred Wisdom fits our understanding, then will it unlock the gate before it is too late? To answer this question, let us see what science and the Qabbala share.

Science offers the physical understanding of all available things. The Qabbala offers the spiritual understanding of all existing things.

The spiritual understanding of all available things comes from the spiritual ether of space. So science can only verify the obvious in the physical realm from the mirror image of the ether of space available through evolution.

"When he prepared the heavens I was there, when he drew a circle on the face of the deep" (Proverbs 8:27). Again, "I" symbolizes the "Sacred Wisdom."

The Divine Infinity Circle

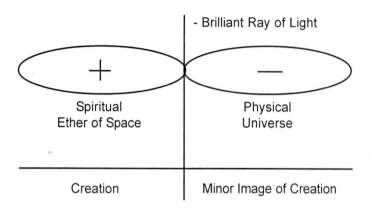

- Brilliant Ray of Light

Spiritual
Ether of Space

Physical
Universe

Creation

Minor Image of Creation

The Mysterious Universe

The human being is a mystery shrouded in a mystery we call the universe. This mystery leads us to yet a deeper mystery we call God. And this three-fold relationship leads us to a deeper yet mystery we call the trinity of life. The universe comes from an unknown source and winds its way toward some unknown end.

tive physical existence. We strive forever more to evolve in time, accomplishing little, yet ignoring the spiritual and mental powers of the consciousness of our intellectual being that could propel us to the unknowable within the spark of that minute glow.

As all knowledge is only relatively true due to the degree of ignorance, wisdom establishes the utilization in accordance with thecircumstances. Use these circumstances and facts, add light from the higher knowledge (the Sacred Code), and with it receive Sacred Wisdom.

The Universe Seen Through Our Eyes

The light reveals to us a universe of four dimensions: length, breadth, thickness and quality. The one encloses or includes the other. But the average person knows only a three-dimensional world, and what is beyond this three-dimensional existence is unknown, if not unknowable, to most. Consequently, the secret of deliverance from ignorance (darkness) is the road to evolution (the expansion of light). And as light grows, so does thought, and with this phenomenon ignorance diminishes.

The world we live in is a world of activity, both positive and negative. It is a world filled with conflict between light and darkness, knowledge and ignorance, good and evil, positive and negative. It is a world of ridiculous revolutions, a cosmos full of chaos.

The universe abhors a vacuum; hence, life is plentiful that fills it, satisfying the cosmic laws. Each separate spark of necessity can never stand still. The darkness looms around it and swallows space if the mere sparks of light (thought) do not continue penetrating the void.

Each true thought flashes a spark of light and is sacred unto this world. When thoughts in the physical realm, the spiritual realm, and the intellectual realm simultaneously flash, a three-fold deliverance is born.

The Principle of Relativity
According to this principle of relativity, value is graded by its worth. The student must pay his or her dues to own a mere speck of a grain of sand of the sand dunes of the Sacred Wisdom. Everything necessitates evolving from the beginning, from the bottom, starting with the seed of the Tree of Knowledge (see Chapter Six).

The Universal Cosmic Laws of Life, the laws by which all life in this universe is regulated, can be likened to the trunk of the Tree. After mastering the basics (the trunk of the Tree of Knowledge), there is little time in the life of the student to conclude the chosen study, the equivalent knowledge of a single branch, encompassing all its facets, deviations, and variations.

The Holy Scriptures teach us the differences among wisdom, knowledge and understanding and how each can be obtained (Proverbs 3:13-20) through the Qabbalistic method. "So they read distinctly from the book, in the law of God, and they gave the sense, and helped them to understand the reading" (Nehemiah 8:8).

With the proper preparation, the Sacred Wisdom can—and should—be made available to everyone. It is the only means with which health, happiness, success, and everlasting life can be obtained.

Chapter 1:
The Sacred Code
1. Corinthians 2:7

The Universal Cosmic Laws
Deuteronomy 29:29

1. The Fourth Dimension of Mathematics

2. The Power of the Word

3. The Sacred Cycles

1. The Fourth Dimension of Mathematics

The values of letters never change.
Numbers cannot default.

Mathematics is the universal principle enabling us to measure everything according to its speed of vibration. It is the universal measurement providing relationship and oneness in all things, proving independence from and relationships with one another.

2. The Power of the Word

A spoken word is immortal!

Every letter of the alphabet owns a specific mathematical place. The Sacred Wisdom regards letters as forms of intelligence. Names are combinations of these letters manifested through speech, expressing thought. Discoveries are recognized through mathematics but expressed through the Power of the Word (language).

The divine forces of intelligence express themselves through the attachment of a name. In every individual, the name motivates the brain cells and with the forces of language creates perfection and conception, making the body respond. The same principle applies to language, revealing the spiritual forces of intelligence and proving the power of the word.

3. The Sacred Cycles

SUMMER   **TRANSITION**   **WINTER**

A rhythmic duplication—nothing is created, only discovered or uncovered. Everything that is, was and will be again.

There is a time to start, a time to see to details, and a time to reap the rewards of expanded efforts. A person's life unfolds in a rhythmic pattern. Through the application of the universal mathematical principle life can be revealed. The following explains the rhythmic pattern starting in everyone's life. It is based on the law of growth, relevant to time. Just as a seed evolves through the stages of growth to reach fruition, a person must live in harmony with the law of growth to reach a successful result.

Mathematics is more than a system of measuring quantity. It represents one of the Universal Cosmic Laws of Life. The Sacred Cyclic Law is the application of mathematics relevant to time. Every person is governed by time—from the beginning to the end of life.

Three basic periods make up the Sacred Cyclic Law: the Starting, the Growth, and the Fruition periods.

Starting Period

The starting period is the beginning of a cycle, a time to commence something and to make changes necessary for expansion. It is the time for action, the time to grow in business and in personal undertakings.

This is a period relating to placing a seed in the ground. The type and quality of a seed planted at a specific time determine the bounty of harvest, and so the actions of a person are equally important in determining the gain.

Growth Period

Everything in life is graded towards its worth. The growth period is a time for determining whether or not the plant warrants further growth. Just as plants have a period when the elements test their roots, a person has a period when he or she must prove the ability to withstand adversities to reap the rewards of his or her efforts.

It is a time in one's private life when a person should strengthen conditions with an aim for the future. This is also a time to strengthen the foundation of a business, delay accepting new responsibilities, and delay making friends, or similar actions that could change present circumstances. Extra care should be taken in personal safety and in health.

Fruition Period

The fruition period is the time when the results of previous efforts are realized. As with plants in nature, we are rewarded relative to the accomplishments set forth in the starting and growth periods. This is the time to reap as you have sown.

The Steps Necessary to Receive the Sacred Code

Revelation 5:1, 4

With the Sacred Code we conceive knowledge, through knowledge understanding, and through understanding all other things. The workings of the Holy Manuscripts are the Sacred Code. The keys that unlock the Sacred Code are:

1. Seeking

2. Truth

3. The First Step

Through seeking we find the truth, which leads to the first step, unveiling the Sacred Code.

Ask, and it will be given to you; seek, and you will find; knock, and it will be opened (Matthew 7:7).

Chapter 2:
Receiving The Sacred Code
Matthew 16:19

There is no actual time or place to receive the Sacred Code. No one is handed a graduation certificate followed by an initiation party. The participant must initiate the steps that will lead to receiving The Sacred Code.

Through Seeking you find the Truth and with the Truth you are able to accomplish the first step (re-birth).

Seeking

For this phenomenon to work, "the seeking" must be genuine.

For me, it all started about 50 years ago, apparently after I evolved enough to realize there is a reason for every effect and a scientific explanation to substantiate the effect through the law of "relativity." I set out to find the scientific formula that, when found, would unveil the mysteries of life and uncover the remedy to all miseries of life, as well.

I realized this was a tall order, though I had no idea it

would take over forty years to receive the answer.

To make a long story short, I began my search in Canada in the '50s with the Roman Catholic Priests, who did not let me read the Bible, who spoke in languages I could not understand, and to whom I was supposed to tell my wrong-doings to rid myself of my sins. I was told all would be forgiven, that I must have faith and pray to the holy mother Mary. Just as all of this makes no sense to me today, it was an utter nonsense to me then, and the furthest thing from my goal. I left the Catholic Church to participate in the Watch Tower of the Jehovah's Witnesses, only to find more confusion.

For five years I tried a number of religious organizations—the United Methodist Church, several Baptist churches, the Anglican Church, First Assembly of God, and finally the evangelists—only to be left in despair. The relation-ships were short-lived and I left each church more con-fused than ever. I did not understand why I was unable to communicate with the Creator who, after all, created us, yet refuses to talk to his created images. All I asked for was the phone number of the Almighty so I might call and talk to Him to resolve many problems, including the dis-crepancies in the Scriptures and the confusion they bring to those who read them.

My strong belief that the Creator existed, combined with my continuous search, finally brought light into the dark-ness. I found the contact who would enlighten me through the information that would unveil the Sacred Code, and through it the Holy Scriptures. The study that followed lasted nine years, but before it was complete I was able to satisfy my burning desire to communicate with the Creator.

The Truth

After a long bus ride from Cold Lake, Alberta, Canada, I arrived in Edmonton on a biting December evening. After a short wait, a United Cab arrived. I quickly got inside the warm car and sat next to the driver. He told me his name was Walter. As we drove Walter casually asked me for my full name-first, middle and last. I hesitantly answered. Then he seemed to be working out something in his mind. A little later, he asked me for my birth date. I started to become a little irritated, not knowing what the unusual questioning was about. I answered anyway, anticipating some unusual analysis. Walter paused, then started to tell me of detailed adversities in my life, one by one. He named personal problems only I could have known. I was completely floored!

I asked Walter how he possibly could know me in such detail, when I only partially recognize myself at any given moment and time. And very calmly, he said, "It is all in your birth date and your name. The birth date is who you should be and the name is who you are, but," he continued, "if 'what you should be' and 'who you are' do not harmonize, do not align, adverse conditions are caused and the imbalance is responsible for the negative influence in your life."

The First Step

Benefiting from the initial steps (seeking and finding truth), I took the mandatory physical rebirth (not the religious interpretation) before commencing with my journey into the unknown. This rebirth aligned my physical creation, or brought it into equilibrium with my spiritual being, which was necessary (Proverbs 11:1) to begin the journey on the narrow path towards everlasting life (Proverbs 1:7).

Technically speaking, "first things first" is the physical and spiritual alignment resulting from receiving the correct name from the Personal Name Analysis; it is through the correct name that the perfect spiritual self (birth date) is capable of expressing itself in a balanced way.

Other forms of rebirth and/or baptism are merely cosmetic at best, serving no merits towards physical and/or spiritual well-being.

The rebirth brought forth a very important alignment with the universe through which I was able to contact the Creator. It was astoundingly easy, yet no one could instruct me--not the clergy, not the generic educational systems. It is amazing what ignorance can do to the populous. The tremendous effort and energy spent by science and evolving societies are in vain. Without the mandatory rebirth, the priceless reward--"the spiritual inheritance"--can never be realized. Society is in dire need of a change.

In the taxi I sat speechless, staring ahead of me and thinking, "If Walter, a complete stranger, can tell me of things only I know, then there must be a powerful force behind this knowledge." And so I asked him of the source of his knowledge. In response, he invited me to stay at his house and meet the source, which could answer all my questions and divert the negative influence presently residing in me, and so stop the destruction.

As I was soon to learn, this "source" was not a person but the Qabbalistic method (Qabbalistic thought) used to esoterically interpret the Holy Scriptures. When mastered, the Qabbalistic thought opens "the book of life" (the Holy Scriptures) to the beholder.

Walter received the Qabbalistic thought from Swami Rai Mohan Dutta, a Holy man from India who represented the Spiritual Cabalah of the East.

Over another nine years I confirmed Walter's findings, with the help of numerous manuscripts/books such as:

- The Vedas of the Sanskrit
- The Volume of the Aural Knowledge
- The Zohar
- The Book of the Intuition
- The Voice of the Earthly Guru
- The Book of the Akashic Records
- The Sepher Yezirah (Book of Creation)
- The Sepher Hatzeruf (Book of Blendings)
- The Sepher Hayuchasin (Book of Genealogies)
- The Sepher Hacasdim (Book of the Chaldees)

- The Sepher Harazim (Book of Secrets)
- The Sepher Hamalbush (Book of Garment)
- The Sepher Hanikud (Book of Dots)
- The Sepher Heedot (Book of Testimonies)
- The Sepher Hayashar (Book of the Upright)

The Results

I am working as a teacher, lecturer and writer at the age of 69. I am fitter than at the age of 35. I love working because I was meant to. I wake up happy every morning and I thank my Creator for giving me this tremendous opportunity to live a life of absolute peace and happiness. I am willing to share this knowledge with everyone who asks for it.

If you desire the life you are meant to live and work to make your life meaningful, tranquil, successful and satisfying, I can help you to satisfy this desire, starting with the Personal Name Analysis at the back of this book. Do "first things first" and everything else will be yours (Matthew 6:33).

From the day of the "Rebirth," remarkable and immediate physical recoveries took place. Healing continued to my fiftieth birthday, when I completely recovered from all my setbacks, ailments and other shortcomings. My life transformed into a life I was meant to live and I became the person I was meant to be from birth.

Chapter 3:
Testing the Sacred Code

Though I didn't know it at the time, in receiving the Sacred Code I was given the tools to analyze life in its entirety—to make changes to anything I could think of. And the most sophisticated technology, man-made laws—even man himself—would be unable to stop me. The average person could never comprehend the enormous power behind those words. I was armed with the most lethal weapon in the universe and I was about to test the earthly knowledge God refers to as inferior.

Every day, I religiously checked my daily calendar forecast to compare the findings with the actual events that took place. Even though I didn't quite understand all of it and I didn't have enough information yet to elaborate the forecasts, they amazed me—each forecast was always right on the button. So I began analyzing everything in sight. I stood in front of posters and analyzed brand names, I analyzed the business names in shop windows—I even analyzed trademarks. When I heard a person's name I'd take pencil and paper and analyze that! I tried to compare the personalities in my analyses with individuals sitting next to me in public transport, or at work, or the cafeteria. I was like a boy with a new toy.

I also began trying to disprove the theory. I would refrain from looking at the daily chart of my calendar forecast, thinking that if I knew what it said I'd somehow influence the events that took place that day. But one day brought a big shock.

Twice and sometimes three times a week I went to visit with Walter. The trip took about thirty-five minutes, taking me from west Edmonton over the river to the northeast side where Walter was living. On that day, I decided I would only look up my forecast if something unusual happened. On the way home, just after turning right into the throughway across the bridge to the west side of town, I was stopped by a motorcycle policeman. I got out of the car and asked him what I'd done wrong, but he continued to write the ticket. After a moment, he said I ran a stop sign and made a gesture with his pen where the stop sign was located. I rushed to the location and sure enough, there it was—a brand spanking new red octagon stop sign. I came by here every time I visited with Walter and never saw a stop sign at that corner. Later, I found out the sign was put up that very day and the policeman was there to enforce it.

The first thing I did when I got home was look at my calendar forecast to see what it said. "Refrain from activity between 3:30 and 4:30 today; adverse conditions in all activities involving motion during this time." I could not believe my eyes! If I'd read my forecast before the day started, I'd have known to exercise caution and would probably not have ended up with a traffic ticket.

Slowly, I began to appreciate ownership of the forecast, and I treasured the formula that made it possible for me to work out my future. I began to think about the power I had at my fingertips—with it, I would be able to change my destiny. The thought that I could be in control of every situation brought goose bumps to my scalp and back. Still, what if the incident with the stop sign had been a fluke? I knew I had to continue to test.

So the next day, I tested it on the way to work. The forecast was perfect for the test: "Excellent for traveling between 12:30 and 1:30 and 3:30 and 4:30." Since everything in life is correlated, the forecast had to be correlated. This means that the reading actually starts at the half hour and reaches its climax at the full hour before it tapers off toward the next half hour, when the conditions for the following hour take over. The year and month had great positive bearing on this day, so the day itself was just right to conduct the test. At twelve noon I traveled my usual route—a 30-mile-an-hour restricted area—over the bridge east. The road I would turn onto was Jasper Avenue, then a four-lane highway that cut straight through the downtown business center. The stoplights at the intersections were synchronized; they turned green if you were traveling at 30 miles per hour.

I came across the bridge at 60 miles per hour and past the stop sign where the policeman had stopped me before. As I flew by, I saw there was no policeman there now! I had to slow down at a corner ahead to make a right turn. Though the light was red, there was no traffic in sight, and

I turned onto Jasper Avenue. I sped up to 50 miles per hour and approached the second traffic light as it turned red. I crossed the intersection—running the red light—but did not encounter a single vehicle! The next light was just ready to turn green when I arrived at the intersection. A red Ford half-ton pickup and a yellow taxi had just cleared the intersection, and as I arrived and crossed the street, the light turned green! In the next half hour, I made six traffic violations and didn't get stopped once.

Trying to Disprove the Theory

Not knowing how my forecasts would impact other people —such as when I flew inside an aircraft—I decided that being alone at the right time was not enough to test the power of the Sacred Code. I also wondered how others would impact my forecast, since in some cases like flying; I was not in control (the pilot was).

During the time I lived in Ketchikan, Alaska, I owned and operated a small construction company. When it was necessary to purchase the materials for a project I would fly to Seattle to shop. First, I estimated the project at actual cost, and then when I was awarded the job I would make deals with suppliers. It was on one of these trips that I was able to put my questions to the test.

I was waiting at the SeaTac airport in Seattle, Washington, to board the flight to Ketchikan, Alaska, when the flight attendant announced, "For those boarding to Ketchikan, there are overcast skies in the area and this flight will very likely have to fly overhead Ketchikan. If this occurs, passengers will be flown to Anchorage at their own expense." Well, this was very discouraging news for everyone, as you can imagine! Around 25 people were destined for Ketchikan, where it rains 90% of the year and has an annual rainfall of around 140 inches. Because of the mountain range, overcast skies often prevent the pilot from getting his bearings when he comes in for the final approach. I was surprised, though, because I'd looked at my schedule and my forecast said there was nothing in my way, that it was an excellent day to travel, especially at the time the plane would be airborne and headed for its destination. I realized this was the very time to disprove the system. For argument's sake I took out my charts and double-checked my analysis; after all, I am just human and could have made a mistake. But I came up with the same forecast.

I went to the group of people waiting for the plane and said, "Anyone traveling to Ketchikan, please board the plane. We will not only arrive on time, but we will land in Ketchikan." When I was asked, "How do you know?" I simply answered, "A little bird told me!" I backed up my forecast by inviting all of them to a free stay in Anchorage should we be diverted. I must have been convincing, since all 25 boarded the plane.

As we approached the destination I saw it was overcast, one solid cloud cover. The plane descended on its final approach, and we soon found ourselves in solid fog. I felt I was being let down badly. I thought, "It was all for nothing. All the effort and all those years spent on the inevitable—and I was wrong." I realized how little strength we had to trust the obvious. But the positive side of me (contrary to the emotional side) told me no man or woman on Earth can mock the Universal Consciousness.

Then I caught a glimpse of a clearing: for perhaps four or five seconds, the landscape below us was visible. And I thought: "If I saw it, so did the pilot!" Sure enough, we broke through the clouds and landed at the Ketchikan International Airport. Everybody gave a sigh of relief. And at the airport, one of the group said to me, "When you go anywhere, let us know; we'd like to come with you!"

A Game of Chance

In Great Britain, the time was just right to win at a game of chance.

I invested in the football pools. Let me explain: the football pool is gambling, but with very good odds. There was always a first prize, as well as dozens of second and hundreds of third prizes each week. The first prize paid on average a million pounds, the second hundreds of pounds and the third tens of pounds. There were around 52 teams playing, and you had to have 8 correct draws out of the 52 teams. For second place, you had to pick 7 correct draws and 1 winner from the guest teams. And for third place, you needed 6 correct draws and 2 winners from the guest teams.

There were 5 or 6 betting companies. Some, like Littlewoods, limited bets to a penny per line, while other companies like Zetters allowed you to bet a farthing per line (a farthing is a quarter of a penny). I chose Zetters because I liked that I was able to bet five pound sterling each week on thousands of lines at a time. On Sunday, after all the teams finished playing, the results came out.

The fifth week I placed bets, there was no first prize winner. What this meant was that the first prize money got divided between the second prizewinners, and if there were no second prizewinners all the money went to the third prizewinners. When I found there were no first prizes I just went to bed, because I had no second prize win, either. What I did have were five third prizes, which would bring maybe ninety pounds. When I went to work on Monday morning, I heard on the news that there were no second prizewinners that week. This changed everything: my five winning tickets had won 458 pound sterling-just over a thousand dollars. It would buy me an airline ticket to Australia, with 400 dollars left in my pocket.

The Darker Side

Arriving in Sydney in December 1959, I found room and board in one of the many spread-out suburbs. The owners had five other boarders, and at breakfast we all gathered at the table and chatted about the day. One morning, we started talking about horoscopes; this of course brought the conversation my way, and I couldn't help but barge in. I explained that horoscopes couldn't really be individualized because there is not enough information in the birth date to offer comprehensive forecasts. A person's name, I told them, must be taken into account for an accurate analysis. So they challenged me by asking if I knew of something that could be of interest to them that day.

I hesitated. I really don't like to prophesize, especially in general terms, and predicting events for someone can be detrimental. But they kept on me about it and finally I gave in. I took the birth date of a guy by the name of Frank, who was very much in a hurry, as he was gulping his food down. I analyzed his year, month and day, hoping for good results. But I found he was in a very bad year, month and day, subject to negative conditions that could lead to bodily harm at best, and accidental death at worst, if he was in motion at a particular hour that morning.

I wondered how I could break this important news to him without upsetting him. I told him to observe caution in all he was doing that day, especially in the morning, as adverse conditions could bring about very bad experiences. I warned him to be extremely cautious between 8:30 and 9:30 in the morning and between 4:30 and 5:30 in the afternoon. But he shrugged his shoulders, refusing to accept the piece of paper on which I'd written those important times.

Frank didn't come home that night. The next morning we found out he'd been run over by a suburban train as he crossed the tracks to catch his connection. He had died instantly at 9:10 a.m.

Needless to say, the owners of the boarding house became suddenly suspicious of me and asked me to leave. They believed I was responsible for Frank's death. Here I was trying to save a person, and I got accused because he hadn't taken notice of my warnings.

But as I came to learn, the response I got wasn't unusual. In Volume II "Perfect Relationships" of "The Sacred Code Series" I describe:

- The day I lost all I owned and ended up in jail because I went against the Sacred Cyclic Laws
- The Power of the Word and the Fourth Dimension of Mathematics
- Why I was married four times but still ended up alone because I went against the Sacred Cyclic Laws
- The day I nearly died trying to disprove the Sacred Wisdom
- In-depth life examples of a fire sign

Chapter 4:
What You Need to Know

The First Forms of Life

All life, visible or not, has to evolve from the densest element and the lowest speed of vibration. The lowest speed of vibration is water, thus all life has to evolve from the ocean. Vibration can be measured through the fourth dimension of mathematics; the result is the quality of the life it forms. After the quality has been established, it becomes visible through the Power of the Word (language) and placed into action through the Sacred Cycles.

The vibrations motivate the brain cells and produce thought, desire, and emotion, and forms the intelligence found in the human mind. Everything that constitutes life is displayed in a name. The combination and balance of these forces generate physical and mental actions and reactions. You are the name and the name represents you. The vibrations of a name are manifestations of intelligence.

The elements are the first forms of life. The "Universal Consciousness" (God) created life, lowering the speed of vibration within our dimension. Material substances apparent to the sight and within our understanding consist of one or more elements. Correlated life forms merge at higher speeds of vibration and create life, each with its relative color, odor, and sound, separate yet correlated. There are no duplications in the sea of life. Thus trying to find another Earth or another humanoid in the physical universe presents the height of immaturity.

The Difference Between the Higher and Lower Speeds of Vibration

The higher the vibration, the faster and more penetrating it is. The lower the vibration, the denser and less penetrating. Similar vibrations do not mix.

This law is applied to thought, which contains a much higher speed of vibration than sound. Thought contains the highest speed of vibration in the human being; it is the platform from which the spiritual speed of vibration begins and accelerates to the spiritual attainment level-the highest speed of vibration in the physical universe.

Language and Mathematics

Mathematics influences and affects all forms of life including animals, birds, and insects, and all things, such as ships, planes, businesses, telephones, house numbers, and addresses. Mathematics influences anything attached to the divine forces of nature, working in and through symbols such as numbers, letters, and language.

Mathematics is the universal language. It is the same in all countries; the value of numbers is basic and cannot change. The symbols of language may change in form and correlation (representing the particular characteristics of the alphabet to which they belong), but the mathematical values of letters and/or symbols are final; they cannot be changed. They represent the letters or symbols used in words or names in every language. To ignore the relationship between language and mathematics would cause chaos in all languages. Only after this phenomenon is understood can the "mystery of the lost word" be solved and the Holy Scriptures be revealed.

The Law of Dimension

Human beings did not create mathematics. It has always existed. It is a fundamental law, discovered through the evolution of the mind. Mathematics is the path to all knowledge. It is the law of dimension. It is one of the Universal Cosmic Laws of Life.

The Complex Human: A Trinity Life Form

The human life form is composed of three beings: the positive (+) mind, the negative (-) physical body, and the spiritual consciousness (thought).

Expression (language) contains different speeds of vibration all harmonizing together. Each level of vibration, whether physical, mental, or spiritual, represents a different octave.

To progress spiritually, increasing the speed of vibration of the physical body and the spiritual mind is necessary. Through correct living habits and the application of the Universal Cosmic Laws that govern the manifestation of the spiritual planes (represented as the 10th, 11th and 12th centers of the spiritual consciousness), the desires of the senses and the mortal mind can be merged into intellect and intellect into spiritual consciousness.

The human being is a conscious being, different from all other life in the universe. No intelligence can be consciously expressed without language. The Holy Scriptures tell us, "In the beginning was the word, and the word was with God and the word was God." The esoteric translation, the Qabbalistic method by which the Holy Scriptures are deciphered, correctly translates the above.

In the beginning there was the word:

The word (The Sacred Wisdom) always was. It was before the creation of the universe and it resides in the spiritual space.

…and the word was with God:

The Sacred Wisdom was with God at the creation of the universe.

…and the word was God:

The Sacred Wisdom is God.

Since the Sacred Wisdom is everything there is, God is in everything there is, and everything there is, is God. Thus the human being is a conscious part of God through the "word," or wisdom expressed in language.

Chapter 5:
Personal Name Analysis
Proverbs 22:1

*A name creates the pattern of thought,
responsible for life experiences.*

Your name will influence the pattern of your thinking. A
balanced name presents the spiritual qualities of self and is
the reflection of the inner qualities a person communicates
to the physical world. Each of your names, combined with
your date of birth, influences your thinking and experiences. Some elements may be similar in nature, accelerat-
ing certain qualities, while others may be opposite, causing a counter-productive reaction.

Today, very few are aware of the importance of the mathematical staging of letters in a name; it is not understood
that an unbalanced name can be mentally and physically
destructive.

The Elements of Name Analysis

A name is the alphabetical choice of letters identifying a
person. The letters of a name have the answers to solving
mental and physical setbacks. Science measures chemicals using formulas. Name analysis measures the human

mind using formulas. A name represents a mathematical combination of the alphabet. This knowledge enables any-one to understand the mind.

To assist you in your self-awareness, this book offers the keys to First Name Analysis. At the end of the book we present you the opportunity to take advantage of a variety of name analyses. Briefly, an entire name analysis includes the following.

Birth Date

A birth date describes the spiritual qualities of a person, those things a person desires through birth. It also identi-fies the character, personality, occupation, and the nature of the person "supposed to be" through birth.

First Name

The first name reveals how much of the inner self is ex-pressed through the name and how much is not, why parts of the inner self are imprisoned, and what a person has to do to change this.

Last Name

The last name describes the desires and needs of the fam-ily. It explains hereditary conditions, and has the power to remove mental and physical breakdowns.

Combined Names

The combined names establish the total anxieties, wants and needs, and are expressed through the first and last names. A person's combined names contain the total positive and negative qualities of the personality, character, and inner nature.

Compatibility Analysis

The compatibility analysis raises the awareness and proves that a happy relationship is far more than just good looks. With this knowledge a person can instantly tell who is or who is not compatible. The analysis describes compatible types of people and explains the importance of compatibility in all areas of life. If a person is married, the analysis establishes his or her shortcomings. By analyzing the name of both parties the compatibility percentages are established.

The First Name Analysis

The first name analysis is one of five separate name analyses available; it is also the most important. The first name analysis personally reflects the person who carries the name. It uncovers ideals, desires, character, personality, and talents.

The consciousness of the human being takes form through vibration and is expressed in language. Vibration is the physical manifestation of the spiritual forces. When the spiritual forces are attached to the human being in infancy through the first name, they stimulate the brain cells in the form of impressions and display the qualities of intelligence.

Every letter has its mathematical position in language. The mathematical relationships of letters in language also represent mathematical positions identifying the speed of vibration. Language separates us from the animal world. Language is the gateway through which thoughts are expressed. Language plays a major role in identifying the Sacred Wisdom in the physical universe.

Letters of a name are categorized into three groups, the practical, sensitive and the inspirational. The letters of a name stemming from the same group share the same qualities, and are most likely compatible with one another.

Each letter of the alphabet owns a unique quality. This quality is identified through the power of the word (language) and is permanent. Desire, personality, character, occupation, vocation and type of nature are identified by the numbers of the letters they represent.

The first step in Name Analysis is associating a letter with a number. The numbers in Formula A1 (below) span 1 through 9 at the right. Everything starts from the west (left) and evolves toward the east (right). You might say no-the sun appears in the east and sets in the west, but in reality we're rotating toward the east! That's why the sun appears in the east: the sun isn't going anywhere—we are. Thus, the numbers begin at the left and stop at 9 at the right. There is no number higher than 9, because once we enter double-digits, the numbers only repeat themselves. 9 is also the perfect number, because it refers back to itself, like a continuous band, a circle or an infinity symbol. No other number can do that. If you take all the numbers from 1 to 9 and multiply or add them, then bring the answer back to a single digit (by adding the result), you get...9! Infinite, perfect, complete.

Formula A1

1	2	3	4	5	6	7	8	9
A	B	C	D	E	F	G	H	I
J	K	L	M	N	O	P	Q	R
S	T	U	V	W	X	Y	Z	

Below the numbers, starting again from the left, we begin with the alphabet, finishing at the number 9 at the right. When we reach number 9, the rest of the alphabet again starts from number 1 and continues to 9 until all the letters of the English alphabet are used up. This is the Sacred Formula A1. All the letters grouped under each number represent the qualities of that number. This brings us to the number identification.

Number Identification

The following introduces the positive and negative aspects of all numbers. If the name is balanced, the positive qualities apply; if not, the negative aspects apply. The birth date is the deciding factor in whether the positive or negative aspects of the analysis will be used.

There are odd and even number qualities. If either type is represented more than twice in the analysis, the name intensifies the quality of the odd or even numbers. In the bottom illustration, the name Nancy is balanced toward the birth date; the positive qualities are used in this example.

Example birth date: *October 5, 1950* (10-5-1950).
Example name: *Nancy*

Reduce the birth date to single digits:

Month: 1+0 = 1
Day: 5
Year: 1+9+5+0 = (1+9) + 5 = 10 + 5 = 15
Reduce 15 to a single digit: 1 + 5 = 6

The birth date October 5, 1950 is reduced to the numbers 1-5-6.

Then, using Formula A1 from the table above, add the numerical qualities to the name Nancy (1-2-3):

Vowels: A=(1)
Consonants: N=5; N=5; C=3; Y=7
5+5+3+7 = 20
20 = 2+0 = (2)
Vowels (1) + Consonants (2) = 1+2 = 3 (1-2-3)

In this equation, we find 1-2-3 contains 2 odd and 1 even number. The birth date 1-5-6 contains 2 odd and 1 even number, as well. If the first name analysis contains the same number groupings as the date the "analysis" is positive.

In the First Name Analysis in this book, we do not use a birth date. In the above analysis we used a birth date to show you whether or not the above name is balanced towards the birth date.

It could be detrimental for anyone to adopt a name without knowing whether or not the qualities of the letters are suitable for his or her birth date. A name is supposed to be an expression of your thoughts. Your thoughts are given to you through your birth date. If the qualities of your thoughts and the qualities of the expression of your name differ, the name prevails and you become the person your name represents. The real you is imprisoned and you reap all the negative aspects of the adopted name such as misfortune, ill health, and unhappiness.

Each time a name is adopted, the qualities of that name will affect the beholder, together and independently. If any of the names are in conflict, the person develops a split personality. We all know that once a word is issued it cannot be taken back—its qualities, good or bad, will act upon the issuer forever. For this reason, never adopt nicknames and never abbreviate a name. On the surface, a name may sound pleasant, when, in fact, the combined qualities of the letters will make life miserable for the unfortunate owner.

To adopt just any name is a serious and risky undertaking.

Only qualified people such as certain Rabbis and people with extensive knowledge of the Sacred Wisdom acquired through the Sacred Code are certified to administer name analysis.

To find out whether or not you have a balanced first name to suit your thoughts, look up Name Analysis at the back pages of this book.

In Volume IV of The Sacred Code Series I describe in-depth the potency and potential of the vibration of life, the joy and reward achieved through absolute balance and the consequences suffered from imbalance.

Chapter 6:
The Tree of Knowledge

Evolutionary Growth Cycle

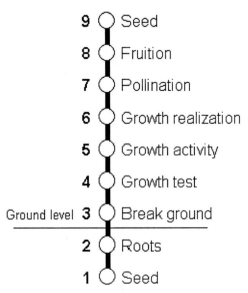

The interpretation of the life cycle from 1 to 9 (below) is in concept the same for every life form in the Universe. Common sense and logic will tell any prudent reader that the interpretations are absolute.

The metaphor of the growth period of the tree in the interpretations is identified through the Three Basic Principles of Life and is in direct co-ordinance with the subject the numerical values represent.

Numbers 1 though 9 in the following sections represent the different types of inner natures. Use the description pertaining to the number to identify the quality of the name. They are: Desire, Personality, Character, Occupation, Vocation, Type of Nature and Physical Weaknesses.

Spiritual Path

Mathematics is the mind or nucleus of language. It is the basic principle of life in its entirety. Mathematics is the fundamental principle through which life "as we know it" was created. Mathematics symbolizes the divine forces of intelligence and is the foundation behind the manifestation of letters in language.

Mathematics alone is able to define the influence affecting life in its entirety. Combined with language, mathematics controls the quality of the human mind identified through the name. Everything in this physical universe is life and is recognizable through the quality in a name, graded by the mathematics influencing the letters in a name. This phenomenon affects animals, birds, business, and anything attached to the divine forces of nature identifiable through the symbols of numbers, and letters residing in names and languages.

The value of numbers is elementary and cannot be changed. Mathematics is universal—for it is the same in all languages and countries. The number one can only have the value of "1". The number two can only be the value of "2" being in the second position, etc.

The symbols in language may change in form and correlation to create other languages such as Hebrew, English, German, Spanish, Chinese, etc. Regardless each letter has its mathematical position in the alphabet of the language it belongs to, and this mathematical position (value) or (spiritual quality) cannot be altered through the change in the form of symbols used. Once the position of numbers and or symbols is known the value remains constant.

The Number Identified

There are basic groups of numbers:

Singular: 1
Dual: 1-1 and
Trinity: 1-1=2

To these three different groups of numbers are attached the qualities (values) which are realized through the second universal principle " The quality of language."

There are three basic types of values to each of the three different groups of numbers: the spiritual value, the physical value and the trinity value. The spiritual values represent the vowels, the physical values represent the consonants and the trinity values are the combination of the added vowels and consonants.

The spiritual values are attached to the spiritual vibration. The physical values are attached to the physical vibration. And the trinity values are attached to the change in vibration.

Let's begin with the singular group this group is sufficient to create your own first name analysis.

Use formula A1.

First, count all the spiritual vowels, bring the total to a single digit figure and read the desire, and personality of that number. Remember the vowel is the spiritual quality of that number and represents the want and needs of its parallel birth date of that person.

Then count all the physical consonants, bring them to a single-digit figure and read the entire segment on that number, pay particular attention to the "character" readout. The consonants represent what other people see in you (true or not).

Finally, add the vowel total and consonant total, bring them to a single digit figure and read the entire description of that number. This would be the true inner self of the person involved the real you.

Formula A1

1	2	3	4	5	6	7	8	9
A	B	C	D	E	F	G	H	I
J	K	L	M	N	O	P	Q	R
S	T	U	V	W	X	Y	Z	

If your name analysis of the vowel interpretation contains
(even or odd) number groups identical to the total of the
analysis then this name is favorable (not necessarily balanced), and the reading will act positively (favorably).

Example: *Susan*
Total vowel count: 4+1=5
Total consonant count: 1+1+5=7
Trinity count: 5+7=12=1+2=3= **123**

The vowel count (5) and the total analysis count (3) are
both odd numbers, rendering them favorable, or positive.
The positive aspects of 5 and 3 appear in the following
pages.

After you have completed your first name analysis, compare it with 1-2-3 in Chapter 9 for accuracy.

In the following pages you will find the interpretation of
numbers from 1 through 9. From each of these values there
are many divisions and scores of deviations. This will serve
you in designing your own first name analysis. The entire
Sacred Code will be presented in future editions of the
series.

1 (ONE) = START

Like the beginning of the Physical Universe, 1 represents the start of all things. In a person born with the equivalent numerical value of 1, the qualities of the inner self (comprised of Desire, Personality, Character, Occupation, Vocation, and Type of Nature) always represent the characteristics of a 1.

The number 1 represents the SEED.

Desire

To lead, to break ground, to reproduce, to seed, to be alone, to pioneer.

Personality

Leader; strong, active, positive, self-confident, candid, he-man, staunch, dependable, unchangeable.

Character

Practical, intellectually powerful, inventive, ingenious, original, strong-willed, true, honest, tends to give orders.

Occupation

Contractor, farming foreman, labor leader, assistant to executives, and manager.

Vocation

Architecture, law, construction, engineering, drafting.

Type of Nature

Physical, deliberate, enduring, independent, self-sufficient, plainspoken.

Controls

Procreation center.

Negative Side
(if name is unbalanced)

Personality

Emotional, not tactful, not diplomatic, aggressive, lacking finesse, awkward, easily embarrassed, blunt, candid, one-track mind.

Type of Nature

Self-centered.

Physical Weaknesses

Eye, ear, nose, sinuses, headaches, loss of hair.

A planted seed of a tree, with proper nourishment, water, and oxygen, develops a root system. This evolutionary process brings us to Phase 2.

2 (TWO) = ASSOCIATION

The second phase of life continues with the development of a root system; this is the equivalent of the numerical value of 2. In a person born with the equivalent numerical value of 2, the qualities of the inner self (comprised of Desire, Personality, Character, Occupation, Vocation, and Type of Nature) always represent the characteristics of a 2.

The number 2 represents the ROOTS.

Desire

To be sociable, to make peace, to teach, to sell, to work with others.

Personality

Tactful, understanding, courteous, pleasant, friendly, agreeable, appealing, loving.

Character

Sociable, lively, conversational, witty, obliging.

Occupation

Diplomat, secretary, demonstrator, salesperson, nurse, teacher, social worker, floorwalker, hairdresser.

Vocation

Diplomacy, music, art, drama, politics, catering, nursing,

hospital care, merchandising, hair care, skin care.

Type of Nature
Peacemaker, diplomatic, generous, easily led, fond of pleasure, relaxing, peaceful, harmonious.

Controls
Fluid center.

Negative Side (if name is unbalanced)

Desire
Not to be alone.

Personality
Passive, sensitive, gossiping, dreaming.

Character
Weak, easygoing, needs encouragement, needs assurance, lacks initiative, lacks determination, lacks system, lacks concentration, hates to budget, lacks self-confidence, lacks leadership.

Type of Nature
Soft, hard to learn, procrastinating.

Physical Weaknesses

Poor blood circulation, stoutness, lack of memory, too much water in the blood, problems with all fluid functions, kidney weaknesses, bladder problems, female disorders.

The revitalization of the seed through the root system enables the plant to develop further and grow out of the ground, reaching Phase 3.

3 (THREE) = EXPRESSION

This is the expression phase of life. In a person born with the equivalent numerical value of 3, the qualities of the inner self (comprised of Desire, Personality, Character, Occupation, Vocation, and Type of Nature) always represent the characteristics of a 3. Through exposure to the elements, the plant experiences forces that determine its fate. Continuing the growth cycle becomes a challenge, but ultimately the plant that survives develops a sturdy, robust trunk, which further enhances the development of its root network. If the plant is underdeveloped at this stage, or ill in any way, it will not survive beyond the test phase.

The number 3 represents BREAKING GROUND.

Desire

To entertain, to express, to break ground, to show off, to dress nicely, to perform, to speak, to act, to entertain, to sell.

Personality

Expressive, spontaneous, imaginative, happy, cheerful, active, high-spirited, humorous, harmonious, performing.

Character

Quick-thinking, talkative, congenial, fortunate, adaptable, optimistic, cosmopolitan.

Occupation

Entertainer, public speaker, artist, salesman, performer, sales manager, advertising manager, display specialist.

Vocation

Entertainment, art, business, sales and marketing, speaking, advertising, literature, acting, merchandising, display.

Type of Nature

Inspirational, witty, positive, forgiving, self-expressive, vital, energetic, thrives upon kindness.

Controls

Fire center.

Negative Side (if name is unbalanced)

Desire

To debate.

Personality

Emotional, scattered, negative, sarcastic, self-centered, argumentative, candid, easily misled, gossipy, forgetful.

Character

Needs encouragement, negative, dislikes monotony, dislikes materiality, dislikes technicality, cannot budget, dislikes mathematics, too generous, foolish, lacks self-confidence, hard to concentrate, full of mischief, lacks punctuality, lacks responsibility, easily hurt, unstable.

Type of Nature

Argumentative, unsystematic, passive, environment.

Physical Weaknesses

Fever in the bloodstream, eczema, dry and itchy skin, liver problems, stomach attacks, gallstones.

4 (FOUR) = TEST

In this phase the plant's strength and endurance are being tested, causing it to stop growing. It is working, developing strength in every fiber of its composition, eliminating infectious areas and strengthening apparent weaknesses. In a person born with the equivalent numerical value of 4, the qualities of the inner self (comprised of Desire, Personality, Character, Occupation, Vocation, and Type of Nature) always represent the characteristics of a 4.

The number 4 represents GROWTH TEST.

Desire

To test things, numerical perfection, system, moderation, to cook, to help.

Personality

Strong, stable, patient, rugged, deliberate, steadfast, steady.

Character

Strong, stable, constant, answering, rugged, neat, thorough, steadfast, trustworthy.

Occupation

Scientist, cook, tradesman, storekeeper, mechanical engineer, doctor, dentist, architect, farmer, clerk, stenographer, machinist, draftsman, editor.

Vocation

Science, mechanics, catering, engineering, architecture, farming, construction, machinery and construction equipment, medicine, medical, surgery, drafting, editing, dentistry, farming.

Type of Nature

Scientific, practical, evaluative, analytical, technical, fundamental, physical, focused, patient, mental, punctual.

Controls

Physical center.

Negative Side (if name is unbalanced)

Personality

Stiff, unbendable, lacks romance, blunt, fussy, not conversational.

Character

Lacks imagination, spontaneous, idealistic, not artistic, not philosophical, not inspirational, not musical, not diplomatic, not expressive, not adaptable, not versatile, lacks confidence, not spiritual minded, not a seeker.

Physical Weaknesses

Stomach and intestinal disorders, constipation, arthritis, rheumatism, boils, growths, blood disease.

Soon the root network is ready with the hardy materials necessary for a quick and intensive growth period.

5 (FIVE) = ACTIVITY

This phase in the life of a plant is the most active. It appears overnight—this little tree shooting toward the sky, growing taller by the day and sturdier by the hour. It branches in every direction, producing little twigs with uncountable numbers of new leaves every day. In a person born with the equivalent numerical value of 5, the qualities of the inner self (composed of Desire, Personality, Character, Occupation, Vocation, and Type of Nature) always represent the characteristics of a 5.

The number 5 represents GROWTH ACTIVITY.

Desire

To travel, to be sociable, to be active, to expand, to be free, to fly, to be physical, to experience new life, to engage in outdoor sports and adventures.

Personality

Constructive, sociable, dynamic, intuitive, active, vital, physical, witty, uses ingenuity, energetic, logical, daring.

Character

Constructive, quick thinker, just, physical, strong, philosophical, gambler.

Occupation

Aviator, sportsman, organizer, traveler, promoter, critic, writer, adventurer, musician, philosopher.

Vocation
Travel, aviation, sports, marketing, music, art, philosophy, writing.

Type of Nature
Constructive, sociable, physical, having premonitions, analytical, philosophical.

Controls
Sound vibration center.

Negative Side
(if name is unbalanced)

Personality
Repressive, overly sensitive, critical, cynical, chaotic, impulsive, antagonistic, discontent, overly optimistic, pessimistic, moody.

Character
Morbid, unforgiving, depressive.

Type of Nature
Frustrated, morbid, destructive, depressive, self-destructive.

Physical Weaknesses

Nervous tension, nervous indigestion, muscular cramps, nervous stomach, ulcer, tension in the solar plexus.
After reaching its predetermined height, the plant stops growing.

6 (SIX) = STABILITY

The plant now uses its stored energy to strengthen the trunk, branches, twigs, bark, leaves and other components. It also reinforces and replaces its vast root network. In a person born with the equivalent numerical value of 6, the qualities of the inner self (comprised of Desire, Personality, Character, Occupation, Vocation, and Type of Nature) always represent the characteristics of a 6.

The number 6 represents GROWTH REALIZATION.

Desire

To counsel, to socialize, to seek, to serve, to help, to balance, to overcome, to speak, to teach, to organize.

Personality

Intelligent, stable, quiet, sure, technical, inspirational, seeking, harmonious, balanced, individual, trustworthy, honest, courteous, affable, understanding, friendly, responsible.

Character

Intelligent, mature, responsible, stable, independent, accumulative, studious, mental, strong character, good taste, proportioning, dependable, trustworthy, honest.

Occupation

Counselor, service industry, musician, orchestra leader, designer, speaker, teacher, lecturer, president, organizer, actor, nurse, matron, principal, philosopher, dressmaker, tailor.

Vocation

Art, industrial, music, designing, speaking, teaching, lecturing, vocal expression, performing, business, economy, politics, nursing, philosophy, tailoring.

Type of Nature

Mature, sexy, stable, positive, mentally quick, independent, analytical, serious, strong maternal instinct, inspirational, creative, balanced, individual, surmount obstacles, trustworthy, just, understanding, philosophical, friendly, dependable.

Controls

Thought center.

Negative Side
(if name is unbalanced)

Personality

Worrying, too serious.

Character

Too serious.

Type of Nature

Worrying, too serious.

Physical Weaknesses

Mental troubles, mental breakdowns, insanity.

Then the growth cycle ends and the plant prepares for thanksgiving.

7 (SEVEN) = REFLECTION

In this phase, the plant displays its extraordinary beauty through the blossoms. It gives thanks to the creator as it rests from the intense growth cycle. It uses its energy to produce a marvel of beauty, scent and richness. In a person born with the equivalent numerical value of 7, the qualities of the inner self (comprised of Desire, Personality, Character, Occupation, Vocation, and Type of Nature) always represent the characteristics of a 7.

The number 7 represents POLLINATION.

Desire

To share, to perform, to study, peace, nature.

Personality

Inspirational, natural, sharing, reflective, placid, peaceful, quiet, gentle, leader.

Character

Natural, mentally powerful, psychic, studious, idealistic, gentle, reserved, logical.

Occupation

Philosopher, writer, horticulturist, actor, real estate dealer, landscape gardener, pipe organist, performer, executive.

Vocation

Philosophy, writing, religion, horticulture, landscaping,

music, performing, drafting, business.

Type of Nature

Inspirational, philosophical, reflective, mathematical, mentally powerful, able to concentrate, placid, peaceful, psychic, idealistic, gentle, reserved, deep thinking, logical, poetic.

Controls

Philosophical center.

Negative Side
(if name is unbalanced)

Personality

Lacking verbal expression, cold, silent, secretive.

Character

Closed-minded, jealous, independent, morbid, too exacting, easily hurt, not revealing feelings.

Type of Nature

Over-sensitive, closed-minded, morbid.

Physical Weaknesses

Palpitation of the solar plexus, respiratory organs, heart, lungs, bronchial problems, tuberculosis, asthma, pleurisy. After the plant recovers from the intoxication of its own beauty, it offers its fruit.

8 (EIGHT) = FRUITION

This is the time for the plant to receive its reward for its hard work. It has survived the fury of the elements; now the work begins to direct the stored energy and the newly manufactured nourishment to create and display the fruit of its labor. In a person born with the equivalent numerical value of 8, the qualities of the inner self (comprised of Desire, Personality, Character, Occupation, Vocation, and Type of Nature) always represent the characteristics of an 8.

The number eight represents FRUITION.

Desire

To lead, to control, to accumulate, to help, to organize, to share, to have justice.

Personality

Leading, understanding, balanced, controlling, ambitious, analytical.

Character

Powerful, stable, balanced, helping, ambitious, just, independent, honest, responsible.

Occupation

Executive, financier, business leader, national leader, banker, broker, realtor, insurance sales, lawyer, contractor, judge, dealer, doctor, financial promoter, writer.

Vocation

Business, economy, finance, analysis, politics, banking, real estate, insurance, law, contracting, trading, medicine, writing, promoting.

Type of Nature

Executive, practical, powerful, just, accumulative, understanding, analytical, honest, charitable, independent.

Controls

Power center.

Negative Side
(if name is unbalanced)

Personality

Stickler for details, materialistic, shrewd, discerning, critical, expensive taste, dishonest, devious, hard, unsympathetic, overly imaginative, blunt, sarcastic.

Character

Unromantic, unsentimental, idealistic, self-centered.

Physical Weaknesses

Generative problems, prostate gland problems, female disorders.

9 (NINE) = COMPLETION

This is the final phase of the evolutionary growth cycle. The ripened fruit is distributed, falling to the ground or being eaten by birds, who take the seeds of the tree to distant places to be washed under the soil and to commence a new cycle of growth. In a person born with the equivalent numerical value of 9, the qualities of the inner self (comprised of Desire, Personality, Character, Occupation, Vocation, and Type of Nature) always represent the characteristics of a 9.

The number 9 represents CYCLIC FULFILLMENT.

Desire

To teach, to speak, to have justice, to sow seeds of wisdom, to find purpose in life, to evolve, to reach for perfection, to complete, to seek, to be a spiritual leader, to be an inspirational guide, to design.

Personality

Sensitive, inspirational, generous, affectionate, understanding, demonstrative, sympathetic, religious, deep, forgiving, dramatic, charming, expressive, loving, feeling, artistic, poetic, charitable, universal.

Character

Idealistic, broad-minded, not vindictive, psychic.

Occupation

Teacher, speaker, lecturer, judge, musician, artist, designer, decorator, writer, doctor, nurse, minister, counselor.

Vocation

Specialist, performer, law, music, art, design, decor, religion, social work, writing, medicine.

Type of Nature

Spiritual, inspirational, sensitive, generous, affectionate, sympathetic, expressive, charitable.

Controls

Spiritual center.

Negative Side
(if name is unbalanced)

Personality

Obsessive, intolerant, intense, selfish, emotional, jealous, sensitive, hot-tempered.

Character

Self-pitying, over-sexed, easily hurt, narrow, small-minded, critical, complaining, gossiping, untidy.

Type of Nature

Dislike systems, dislike monotony, possessive.

Physical Weaknesses

Nervous seizures, nervous disorders, hysteria, tension, epilepsy, fits, shaking of the muscular system, unconsciousness, strokes, St. Vitus's dance, nervous breakdowns.

Chapter 7:
The Tree of Life

Blessed are those who do his commandments,
that they may have the right to the Tree of Life
and may enter through the gates into the city.
Revelation 22:14

The Tree of Life plays the ultimate role in the life of the spirit. It outlines the spiritual evolutionary growth in the life cycle. Through knowledge, evolution in wisdom is possible. Through growth in wisdom, the evolution of the Tree of Life is accomplished. Arriving at the twelfth level of the Tree of Life is the ultimate achievement of the earth-bound spirit, which is rewarded with Spiritual Inheritance.

The Twelve Centers

The human being is identified in the Guide Book of Life as the Tree of Life. The Tree of Life contains twelve centers:

12.....Third Spiritual Level (Spiritual Consciousness Level)

11..2..Spiritual Level

10..1..Spiritual Level

 9......Spiritual Center

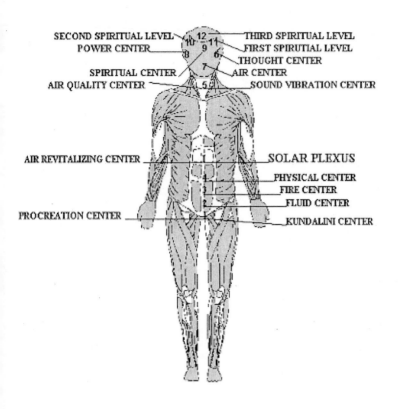

8......Thought Center

7......Air Center (Philosophical Center)

6......Power Center

5......Sound Vibration Center

Solar Plexus (Air Vitalization Center)

4......Physical Center

3......Fire Center

2......Fluid Center

1......Kundalini Center (Procreation Center)

The Tree of Life illustrates the tasks the individual faces in order to evolve from the lower emotions and attain Spiritual Inheritance.

1. The Kundalini Center

The Kundalini Center is where the "mana" of the brain is manufactured to nourish the brain cells. This backbone liquid is also applied to the reproductive functions, creating new physical life. If the mana is wasted through excessive discharging of the sex organs, the liquid is prevented from reaching the brain cells, the mind is starved of food, and the ability to think deeply is relinquished.

This is the first of the four emotional centers of the Tree of Life, described by the Holy Scriptures: "and the beast was like a Lion, and the second beast like a Calf, and the third beast like face as a man, and the fourth beast like a flying eagle…" (Rev. 4:7).

This identifies the four lower emotional centers, which, when not overcome, lead to spiritual death.
Emotional urges must be curbed before evolution in wisdom can begin. In most cases, half the lifetime passes before evolution can begin. This is sad, because there is not enough time left to evolve to the attainment level before the rest of the physical life has been expended.

2. The Fluid Center

All the liquids in the body are controlled by this emotional center and the conversion of solid food intake. We all know how hard it is to conserve the food intake.

Abstaining from alcohol, coffee, and other detrimental substances is of utmost importance. They fuel the negative impulses, invigorating emotions that keep the individual trapped in the lower four centers. The four emotional centers work together, and in unison they can prevent a person from escaping, forcing the individual to revolve in the lower four centers. They are the four beasts the Bible describes in the book of Revelation, and evolving from them is a royal battle.

3. The Fire Center

This emotional center is in control of the solids of the body, muscles, tendons, skin, and bones. The emphasis is directed toward how we look and the things we do to make ourselves look better, including the various physical exercises employed to make us feel better, as well. It is hard to stop idolizing the body in general, and self in particular.

4. The Physical Center

This, the last physical center, controls the detrimental lower emotions. It controls the nervous system, which has a wide range of power over the way we feel, sense, and touch. It is the most difficult power to break away from the first center. It determines how we feel toward others, including our indulgence in sex, how we react through sensing things, and how we judge the emotions of the other three lower centers.

If the mind is used in place of the lower emotions, it is easier to control the habits of the four lower emotional centers: with the power of the mind, it is a snap to move away from them. But as long as a person is ruled by emotion, there is little chance to break away from certain death.

Solar Plexus Center

The solar plexus serves many functions and is located at the center of the body. First, it is the place where Christ died after the arrival from the Ether of Space and where he remains until resurrection. Second, it is the center where the individual evolving from the lower four centers revives Christ. This is accomplished by the spiritual recognition and the physical baptism. The spiritual recognition is the recognition that Christ has come in the flesh and is here to forgive the sins of the beholder. The physical baptism is accomplished by practicing "first things first"—aligning spirit and body in equilibrium with the universe. This is the re-birth of the human spirit.

Third, it is the first center to rejoice from terrible experiences and torment. No longer will there be grief and horror. There will be no turning back to the emotional disposition. For the first time the individual is at peace and lives in tranquility. From this point, Christ will be in control of the individual and together they journey from center to center, evolving to the highest level in the Tree of Life as the lower four emotional centers calm down and unconditionally obey orders received from the individual. For the first time the individual's mind controls the lower body. Fourth and finally, this center is the "Air Revitalizing Center." Each breath can be locked and held inside the lungs and pushed down by force, revitalizing the air so the person becomes intoxicated and can pass out. The degree of regained energy can be monitored by nerve sensitivity. People who "recharge their battery" this way never move a muscle when a cannon is discharged a few feet away. Another extreme example of a recharged battery is when a person walks in the snow naked at subzero temperatures without complications of any kind afterward.

5. The Sound Vibration Center

Controls the vocal cords.

6. The Power Center

Controls the brain.

7. The Air Center (Philosophical Center)

Controls the lungs.

8. The Thought Center

Controls the mind.

9. The Spiritual Center

Controls spirituality.

10. The First Spiritual Level

Attainment preparation.

11. The Second Spiritual Level

Controls attainment preparation.

12. The Third Spiritual Level (Spiritual Attainment Level)

Chapter 8:
Letter Years

Tracing the Events of Your Life

You can find the years of dramatic and/or outstanding developments in your life by analyzing the "letter years" in your name. Let's take the name *Susan* and attach the numerical equivalent to each letter using Formula A1:

Formula A1

1	2	3	4	5	6	7	8	9
A	B	C	D	E	F	G	H	I
J	K	L	M	N	O	P	Q	R
S	T	U	V	W	X	Y	Z	

$$(S)1\text{-}(U)3\text{-}(S)1\text{-}(A)1\text{-}(N)5$$

Reading from the left, the second number (3) and the second to last number (1) play a special role; they are the vowels of the name. These have special impact on the desires, moods and other emotions affecting your personality.

Each letter year lasts for the duration of its mathematical equivalent: the (1) lasts for one year, the (3) for three years and so on. As we begin the analysis, the first number (1) represents the readout from the formula. Then we add the (1) to the (3) next in line and we get a (4). The (4) represents the age 4, when this person has another outstanding experience. Take the second number (3) and present the readout. This experience will last for 3 years. Then we add (1) next in line to the (4) and we receive (5); at five years of age this person has yet another outstanding experience and this time that of (1) again. Take the readout for the (1) from the formula. The next number is another (1) and we have 2 consecutive years of an outstanding experience (of 2 years). Add the (1) to the five and you receive (6). At the age of 6, this person has an outstanding experience of a numerical equivalent of a (5). Add the (6) and (5) together and this person has the next outstanding experience at the age of 11 years.

When you reach the end of the numerical equivalent of the letters in your name, start all over again until you reach the age of 81 years. According to the Sacred Wisdom, 81 years is the life expectancy of the human being—27 years 3 times—the trinity cycle.

- The first 27 years is the learning or receiving cycle

- The second 27 years is the production cycle

- The third 27 years is the teaching or giving cycle

. 1. For easy calculation, add the letter years together and write them under each letter.

2. Read the numbers vertically from each letter and at a glance you have all the (age) years of the person's outstanding experiences.

With *Susan*, take the (1) of *S* add it to the (3) of *U* and you receive (4).

Take the (4) total and add the (1) of the second *S* and you receive (5).

Take the total (5) and add the (1) of *A* and you receive (6). Take the total (6) and add the (5) of *N* and you receive a total of (11).

Follow the above example until you reach the age of 81.

1	3	1	1	5
S	**U**	**S**	**A**	**N**
1	4	5	6	11
12	15	16	17	22
23	26	27	28	33
34	37	38	39	44
45	48	49	50	55
56	59	60	61	66
67	70	71	72	77
78	81			

The entire letters years of SUSAN consist of a 1 year, a 3 year and a 5 year.

The 1 year in SUSAN is repeated three times and the remainder one time.

We start with the 1 year, combining all three times: the *S*, *S* and *A*.

The read-out is as follows:

1-5-6-11-12-16-17-23-27-28-34-38-39-45-49-50-56-
60-61-67-71-72-78-81.

At the above ages and lasting for one year each, you are influenced by strong urges for a vital change. A dominant force that will make you express and feel more positively governs you. These times are trying and cause headaches from tension. In times like these you always make your own decisions and act upon them aggressively and independently. You lack verbal expression, and because of it, you could be tactless and short.

4-15-26-37-48-59-70-81

At the above ages and lasting for three years each, very favorable times come your way. Active conditions create congenial and sociable influences in your life with a greater opportunity for verbal and emotional expression through music, art, drama and your affections. It is a fortunate period but not a stable or accumulative one. It is best expressed as a happy-go-lucky time in which things come and go without worry. You can always look back to these years with happy memories, depending upon the degree of emotion in your inner nature. There is a strong tendency to overeat sugars and starchy foods, affecting the functions of the liver, causing a weak back or skin eruptions.

11-22-33-44-55-66-77

At the above ages and lasting for five years each, you enter a period of change, action, and turbulence, and you have many educational experiences. Much can be accomplished, but at a cost. It is a wonderful period in which to expand your endeavors, including your business affairs. These periods include travel, relocation, and other personal changes. You are high strung at these times and should take time out to relax as much as possible. Things can be chaotic and disturbing influences can affect the solar plexus and stomach. It is an educational period that often brings a change of environment. You are inclined to act upon emotions rather than by intellect and sound reasoning.

Use the preceding example of *Susan* to find the numerical equivalents for your name. Discover the Events of Your Life in the following Letter Year Tables.

Complete Letter Year Table

Letter Year (1) = A J S

The value of 1 represents a one-year period.

When you come under the influence of this letter, you know the depth of your needs and desires. You must realize independence from others. You dislike interference from individuals around you; this interference stops you from performing, and usually it happens when you are in the middle of something.

You are gifted, bringing to life beautiful creations. You come up with ideas that others should pay attention to; they don't know what they are missing. You have the ability to lead in all of your endeavors. Few people recognize your natural abilities. You are self-reliant and possess unlimited perseverance. You are strong-willed; nobody should dare to oppose you. You are very good with your hands, and thus you can show others your hands-on capabilities. You are a strong lover with a lot of endurance.

However, don't let these abilities go to your head. Be merciful and show compassion towards the unfortunate. Curb your language. You are apt to speak as you feel, and this is not the way to make your point. Yes, you have strong feelings about things and it is very hard for others to penetrate your standpoint. If you can't bear the incompetence around you, go swimming or embrace nature in other ways. Do the things that come naturally and you will emerge a new person.

Letter Year (2) = B K T

The value of 2 represents a two-year period.

You have a difficult time trying to cope with things. This is especially hard on you, because you love to be with people. You are devastated by the thought of being alone. You love peace and harmony. You are there when others need help. However, be careful about giving financial assistance to others. You don't want to end up short. Remember, you love comfort and peaceful living. Don't let others destroy this.

You perform best in situations among other people and when working with others. Associate with others to find out what makes them tick. You need mental interaction to learn about others, so you can be tolerant and understand their hearts and minds. You dislike turmoil, war, and atrocities. You would be an excellent negotiator in solving problems; a born diplomat. You are a refined person and your inner feelings are placid. This, however, gets you into trouble. You want to take it easy too often. You must discipline yourself for an active life so you can keep what you have. You don't like to face issues, but there are things in life only you can solve, and you have to stand up to them. You must fight back to keep your position. Running away will only make you lose the things you yearn for. You hate to take constructive criticism, but if you don't listen to constructive critics, you will fall to unrecoverable depths.

Letter Year (3) = C L U

The value of 3 represents a three-year period.

Although you inspire others in many ways, you should target your ambitions towards a more rewarding benefit, such as teaching Divine Wisdom to the less fortunate. You are an inquisitive soul and finding the Divine Wisdom should be no problem for you. Your sensitive nature gets the better of you, and can experience detrimental consequences if you don't control your compassion for others. Your high ideals are fueled by your inspirational inner nature. Your personal desires, wants and needs should be balanced towards the wants and needs of others. You have a hard time doing this, but your rewards for this are far greater in perspective than acting to the contrary. On the other hand, if you don't take heed, you only become unhappy and emotionally unstable. Your love for others is overwhelming, and if you go to the extreme you can get hurt. It is wise for you to walk the golden path right down the middle to make your life a beautiful experience. Enhance your natural gifts in music, art, and drama. Develop them to greater heights for additional tranquility.

Letter Year (4) = D M V

The value of 4 represents a four-year period.

You are meticulous in your endeavors. You can create art and sculpture with your hands. Develop your mental talent to become a great mathematician. Be careful when using your precise mental and physical abilities; they may be intimidating to others. Show sympathy towards the unfortunate. Ease up on demanding written proof of the elementary. Make it easy on yourself, and share your practical, mechanical, and technical abilities with others to reap great rewards. Use your analytical nature, and bring into form the secrets of nature's law. As you proceed with this, your own life management will be enhanced. Look at life as a great prospect and overcome the mundane existence of everyday tasks. Don't let anyone rush you into completing your work, or it will not end successfully. By nature, you are skeptical. Don't make it obvious to other people. You would make a great scientist, one who proves things through slow, meticulous and steady efforts. Accept positions in which you can excel in your work freely.

Letter Year (5) = E N W

The value of 5 represents a five-year period.

During this five-year period it is hard for you to be in one location for any length of time. You desire constant change in everything. It is not easy for you to settle down with children, or to go to the same job every day. You travel more than other people. For you to succeed, you must concentrate. Focus on one object at a time. Put things away with thought behind their purpose and function; if you don't, you will have a mess on your hands and won't be able to find anything. Think of the greater aspects of life and have faith in your keen ability to find them. Control your emotions, and don't let them get the better of you. Don't express and respond to your feelings. Let your thoughts rule them. All things crossing your path have to be challenging. It is important for you to be with a compatible partner in marriage and at work. If you are not compatible, you will both pay the consequences. It is best for you to accept a position in which frequent travel is possible. A position as a pilot would be very suitable, or a position in which you will be given freedom of thought to initiate, develop and promote new ideas. Pursue your inner feelings to seek and find the mysteries of the unknown. If you start early in your life, you will get to know the reason behind all things. The challenge of the unattainable will give you tranquility.

Letter Year (6) = F O X

The value of 6 represents a six-year period.

In this period you have the great ability to look into your life and see ahead to structure your personal participation to your advantage. It is your desire to work with people. You are great management material, and if you hire compatible work groups to work with you, your success is assured with half of the effort spent. Your inner desire to help others benefits all participants. You have a great sense of responsibility, and a desire to care for the needs of others. You have the potential to develop foresight. You are positive and have the mental power to handle all situations that come your way. You possess a strong sense of self-assurance and confidence. Be tolerant in your decision-making involving others, so that you do not develop a superior attitude. Your desire to assist others can have negative results if you assume too many responsibilities and make too many decisions on behalf of others. Early in your life, you yearn for family and home. Your priority is to settle down early. This gives you the sense of accomplishment and security you need in order to find peace and happiness.

Letter Year (7) = G P Y

The value of 7 represents a seven-year period.

You are a very sensitive individual during this period, and you feel more than words can express. Your reflective inner nature craves harmony, refinement and peace. People have problems understanding your reserved disposition. They don't know you are having difficulties expressing yourself verbally. To help overcome your self-consciousness, congregate with others and give graciously. In the meantime, you have to deal with others the best way you can to expand your friendships. Little gestures thrill you, and a single rose can do wonders for your soul. It is your purpose to unveil the mysteries of life, and with your literary ability you are able to document your findings. You are a natural writer and philosopher. Your greatest relaxation and peace is experienced in the outdoors, close to nature. You have to evolve to understand life in general, and people in particular, to appreciate and overcome your intense sensitivity.

Letter Year (8) = H Q Z

The value of 8 represents an eight-year period.

You love people and you want to be among them. You don't like to be shut out, you deserve recognition, and you are a hard worker. You have great leadership and management abilities. Your talent to organize intensifies your management skills. Early in life, you sense the need to be an individual and establish financial independence. You are born to chase the dollar, and you are very successful. You complain about the hard work, however it may be to justify your success. You assume too many responsibilities on behalf of others. Your inner feelings urge you to establish a universal concept to assist others through justice. Congregate with others and don't discuss money matters, because others find it boring.

Letter Year (9) = I R

The value of 9 represents a nine-year period.

In this period of your life you are a very inspirational soul with a love of music, drama and art. You feel you are born to inspire others, and to make them rise above their miseries and doubtful existence. Your greatest gift is to give to others, so you must be careful not to give away the physical comforts that you cherish so much. You must focus on the broader picture, and not get lost in personal desires that bring you unhappiness and instability. Your sympathetic nature must be balanced against your emotions and not overrule your better judgment. You are a great marketer; selling wisdom is no challenge to you. You love the finer things in life and often spend too much time and money on how you think you should look. Developing your musical, artistic and acting abilities could bring you fame and great satisfaction. Although you love wealth and fame, you long for family, home, and parenthood.

The influence of nine is of an emotional nature. Unless allowed constructive expression through creative engagement, you become emotional and cause personal problems, embarrassing emotional situations, and shattered ideals or affection. If you have the knowledge of the Universal Principle, it can be a very full and happy period of accomplishment. In the lives of almost all people, it is an unsettled time, with mental and emotional adversity prevailing for four years. Tests and negative conditions occur during the fourth year. A major personal problem is usually experienced during the ninth year.

Chapter 9:
Numerical Equivalents

The First Name Analysis

The First Name Analysis consists of three factors:

- The Plane of Mind
- The Outer Self
- The Expression of the Plane of Mind

The Plane of Mind: Vowels

There are six planes of mind in the English language (sometimes seven), and they are endowed to the entire English-speaking population of Earth. The seventh vowel is the consonant "y," used only if there are no "real" vowels present in a name.

The birth of a person regulates the issuing of the type of vowel(s) in the Plane of Mind of a name.

The Outer Self: Consonants

The outer self-expresses the person you are in the eyes of others.

The Plane of Mind Expression: Value of Vowels and Consonants

Expresses the values of the inner nature, character, personality, desires and vocation.

Instructions for Finding the Number Combination for Your Name

Example name: *Susan*

Formula A1

1	2	3	4	5	6	7	8	9
A	B	C	D	E	F	G	H	I
J	K	L	M	N	O	P	Q	R
S	T	U	V	W	X	Y	Z	

1. First add the vowels U and A = U+A = 3+1 = 4

   The vowel total = 4

2. Then add the consonants S and S and N = S+S+N = 1+1+5 = 7

   The consonant total = 7

3. Finally, take the vowel total 4 and the consonant total 7 and add them together:

   4+7 = 11; further reduce this: 1+1 = 2

   The equation total = 2

4. Place the vowel total 4 first, the consonant total 7 next, and the equation total 2 last:

NUMBER COMBINATION = 472

5. Read the First Name Analysis description for 472.

Note: Your answer must always be a single digit. If you have more than a single digit, add them again until you obtain a single digit (see number 3 equation).

A CD version of the following is available.

1 1 2 COMBINATION for: "ANN" or "MAX" or equivalent

You are an individual, original in your ideas, positive, candid, and witty when provoked. You persevere in your actions. Your desire is to lead and pioneer, to navigate uncharted waters, and both your pragmatism and creativity express individuality. You are a social climber and your diplomatic talents are employed primarily at the social level. You are positive, you dress nicely, and you speak well. You are tactful and smooth.

The negative influences of this name make you self-centered and limited in thought, passive in your actions, lacking depth and inspiration. You are ready to tell others what to do, but you do not follow your own advice. You are not easily inspired.

Your physical weaknesses would appear in one or more of the following: your eyes and sinuses; headaches; loss of hair; poor teeth; ear and nose problems; kidney disorders; fluid function interruptions; and female problems.

1 2 3 COMBINATION for: "AMY" or "ART" or equivalent

You desire new experiences, you are independent, and you need to be free. You are a practical person, though inventive in your ideas and original in thought. You love the outdoors and you find peace and tranquility in nature. You love to challenge the natural forces with your physical strength.

In business, your success lies in the practical aspect of things. You are a born leader and you work best in an environment in which your perseverance, self-reliance and leadership qualities can be introduced. Others look at you as a peacemaker, able to bring people together and create peace and harmony. They find you a sensitive, refined person who opposes turmoil and hardship.

Sometimes the will of others overwhelms you and you wish to be the person they think you are. Because you are a born performer, you could easily pretend to be what others want; you love to display your inspirational and creative talents through others.

You are systematic and your natural talents can be presented in an orderly fashion. You have a strong natural sense of harmony in all matters. Your compassion for people could bring them a great deal of inspiration. You are happy and optimistic in your outlook, and you can maintain this positive disposition through constructive thought and action, keeping at bay negative beliefs regarding your personal performance. In business and in your personal life, you love to entertain and express yourself explicitly. Selling new, groundbreaking products excites you.

You dress immaculately, like to show off on stage, and you perform best in large crowds. You have an active and cheerful personality, and you are always performing. Your quick thinking rescues you from imminent disaster. Your imaginative powers are diverse and can go overboard. Your devotion to your loved ones is spontaneous and your outlook on life is cosmopolitan. Your adaptable character keeps you employed. Your pleasant demeanor can be laced with humor and you thrive upon kindness. You are a very independent person, with a powerful and positive mind and an extremely active body.

Everyone loves your artistic talents. Your power of expression makes you an excellent sales person. Marketing for you is second nature. Your good disposition proves an advantage. Your talkative nature brings you a lot of friends and acquaintances. In a nutshell, you are good-natured, creative, talkative, sympathetic, affectionate, and you like to sing.

1 3 4 COMBINATION for "DAISY" or "DAVID" or equivalent

You are inspirational, compassionate, and creative, and you have a strong sense of harmony in all matters. Others see in you a happy and optimistic person with an overwhelmingly positive outlook on life. They believe you are devoted to your loved ones and your life is effortless. You seem to have a highly active and cheerful personality.

In fact, you have the potential to be a homebody and your cooking is second to none. You pursue the technical and mechanical side of life. You are skeptical and demand scientific proof before you accept something as fact. You count the pennies when given change. While others fail when performing monotonous tasks, you are just beginning. You love tedious projects and your patient, slow and steady efforts always win in the end. Your analytical ability helps you access nature's innermost secrets. You lose sight of the overall picture easily; thus you should concentrate on concept. You excel in work in which you can deal with the details of an operation and/or numerical perfection. You have a strong, stable, rugged personality and a steadfast, stable character to match. You are trustworthy, deliberate in your planning, and firm in your decisions. You are thorough, neat, steady, punctual, patient, and technical.

You desire new experiences, and you may become aware of your independent character and the need to be free. You are a practical person, though inventive in your ideas and original in thought. You love the outdoors and you find peace and tranquility in nature. You love to challenge the natural forces with your physical strength. In business, your success lies in the practical aspect of things. You are a born leader and you work best in an environment where your perseverance, self-reliance and leadership qualities can be introduced.

You can develop musical and artistic abilities but prefer system, planning and action. You enjoy doing things with your hands, steadily plodding along in your hard work. You like to be independent in your business, and you are patient in your outlook on life. You have the ability the invent things along scientific lines. You have the tendency to be headstrong, stubborn and domineering. Through lack of imagination, your one-track mind sometimes gets you into trouble. You are not versatile in thought, thus must have tangible proof in order to visualize.

1 4 5 COMBINATION for "LISA" or "FRANK" or equivalent

You give the impression of being a well-educated individual with technical and mechanical abilities. People think you are a homebody and love tedious projects. You show that you are trustworthy and steadfast, deliberate in your planning and firm in your decisions. In reality, you have a keen sense of truth and logic. You feel a lot more than you express. Sometimes this is a setback if you do not control your impulsive reactions. Your inner urge for change and travel is almost unbearable. You constantly seek greener pastures. You start many things that you have problems finishing; you start with great interest but quickly lose it if the project becomes too monotonous or detailed. Your natural desire to find the reasons behind the forces of nature awakens your interest early in life. You must control your verbal expressions through self-discipline to curb intolerance, criticism, and impatience.

You desire freedom of thought and to be able to think without the interference of others. You would make a great traveling salesperson or aviator. You would also excel in work in which you have the freedom of thought and action and can promote new ideas and/or products. You are constructive in your efforts, intuitive, dynamic, and sometimes witty. You desire the experience of new and uncharted islands, educate yourself through new experiences, and introduce your new concepts to others. You are inventive in your ideas and original in your thought. You possess strong sexual desires, and your feelings supersede your actions. You can be blunt when aroused and sarcastic when provoked. You love the outdoors and you find peace and tranquility in nature. You love to challenge your physical strength with the forces of nature. In business, your success lies in the practical aspect of things. You are a born leader and you work best in an environment in which your perseverance, self-reliance, and leadership qualities can be introduced. All in all, you are a very ambitious person, action and motion personified. Individuals like you leave home early and make their own way. You are a positive person with great initiative and drive.

You strive to be your own boss, depending on the degree of balance in your complete name. If you don't control your emotions you can be dominant, self-centered, and sarcastic. You have problems relaxing. You only find pleasure in ordinary congeniality.

1 5 6 COMBINATION for: "SALLY" or "SAM"or equivalent

Others are given to believe you are constantly looking for better places to go. You seem to be scattered in your actions, starting many things you can't seem to finish. You wish to find and experience new and uncharted islands, educate yourself through new experiences, and introduce your new concepts to others. You establish your identity through individualism. If your name is given to you at birth, early in life you become aware of your independent character and the need to be free from the interference of others. Basically, you are a practical person, inventive in your ideas, creative through your hands and original in your thought.

You possess strong sexual desires, and your feelings supersede your actions. You can be blunt when aroused and sarcastic when provoked. You love the outdoors and you find peace and tranquility in nature. You work best in an environment in which your perseverance, self-reliance and leadership qualities can be introduced. You take on responsibility for others. You take care of the needs of other people. Organization is your defining characteristic…you are able to organize your business and personal life in your sleep. People can come to you to consult about general or personal problems. They always receive an abundance of useful information. You are gifted with the ability to balance the art of living. Nothing can deter you from getting what you want. Your social activities are numerous and you are more than welcome to attend and lead social activities in your community. Your intelligence and trust-worthiness is highly respected. Your quiet, stable personality is only superseded by your understanding and friendly disposition. You are responsible, honest, and inspirational to others. You have excellent taste.

You are studious, mature, and like to do business independently. You tend to accumulate and take responsibility for your actions. People can rely on your judgment and depend upon your promises. No matter how others perceive you, you are an astute, stable person who is sure of his or her actions. You have many inspirations, some with a technical flavor. You are attracted to a harmonious, balanced life. Many appreciate your trust-worthy and honest character. You have a courteous, understanding personality, with an affable, perceptive nature.

1 6 7 COMBINATION for: "SYLVIA" or "MARK"or equivalent

To others you appear a responsible person who tends also to take on responsibility for others. It looks like you fulfill the needs of others; people consult with you about general or personal problems and always seem to receive an abundance of useful information.

You are organized, especially in business. Nothing can deter you from getting what you want. Your social activities are numerous and you are more than welcome to attend and lead social activities in your community. But you really express deep feelings and thoughts towards others. You have a natural gift for reflecting on your inner nature and you seek out the mysteries of life in the universe. You are a natural philosopher and love to dwell in the depths of religion. Your sensitivity is acute…you can sense things before they become realized. You can look at a person and know what he or she is about to say before they say it, and this makes others indifferent towards you; they think you are secretive and stuck up. You are quiet and it seems that you go about things deep in thought.

You are refined and love the outdoors. Little things make you happy. A single flower can arouse deep appreciation while a bouquet of roses would leave you cold. You love nature in its natural state and find peace and harmony among the trees, rolling hills, and blue skies.

You can sense a lot more than you may be able to express, causing you to retreat from normal activities while being misunderstood by others. Your idealistic nature is surpassed by your studious, psychic personality and topped by your natural, gentle ways. You should educate yourself about your emotional shortcomings.

You wish to educate yourself through new experiences and introduce your new concept of religion to others. You should establish your identity through individualism. Early in your life, you become aware of your independent character and the need to be free from the interference of others. Basically, you are a practical person, inventive in your ideas, creative with your hands, and original in your thought. You can be blunt when aroused and sarcastic when provoked. You love the outdoors and you find peace and tranquility in nature.

You love to challenge your physical strength with nature. In business, your success lies in the practical aspect of things. You are a born leader and you work best in an environment in which your perseverance, self-reliance, and leadership qualities can be introduced.

1 7 8 COMBINATION for: "HELEN" or "BRIAN" or equivalent

You are a practical person, inventive in your ideas, creative with your hands, and original in your thought. Your feelings supersede your actions . . . you can be blunt when aroused and sarcastic when provoked. You express the depth of your feelings towards others and you possess strong sexual desires.

Others see you as a philosopher who loves to dwell in the depths of religion. You desire new dramatic experiences, wishing to go places no one has been before and use new experiences to build your future. Introduce these new experiences to others so they may learn. Early in your life, you become aware of your independent character and the need to be free from the interference of others, and it is your duty to establish your identity through individualism.

You love the outdoors and find peace and tranquility in nature. You love to challenge your physical strength with the forces of nature. In business, your success lies in the practical aspect of things. You are a born leader and you work best in an environment in which your perseverance, self-reliance, and leadership qualities can be introduced. To organize and assume responsibility for others is your defining drive. You are able to organize a business or your private life with ease. The yearning for financial independence is predominant in your life, thus you only accept positions in which you have the power and control over commodities and decision-making.

Your inner nature is giving; you like to share and help the needy. Your ambition seems to overcome obstacles with ease, and your endless energy and stamina allow you to forge ahead to reach your goals. Your analytical mind quickly assumes responsibility and sometimes takes calculated risks when winning is in your favor. Your solutions are practical and versatile, your powerful nature focuses on accumulation, and your independent character is charitable and honest.

However, this name limits your mental capabilities and the divine structure of your spiritual qualities.
If you'd like to make a change to your name, please read the information on Name Analysis in the last pages of this book.

1 8 9 COMBINATION for: "DINAH" or "STAN" or equivalent

People see a great organizer in you, a person who cares for others. They see an ambitious, charitable, honest, and well-to-do person. You inspire others through wisdom and guide them onto the path leading to their spiritual inheritance.

Through your personal evolution, you find the purpose in your life and in the lives of others. Your advanced inspirational nature is a natural endowment you are to share with others. Early in life, you recognize the need to search for truth and the desire to give this wisdom to the masses. You are an inspirational guide to many and your need to strive for perfection makes you the expert in the field. You leave the audience spellbound when you speak.

Your sensitivity demonstrates your compassion for others and your generosity alleviates their suffering. You do not hold grudges and you are affectionate with the needy. Your deep religious feelings receive clarity through evolution of self. You begin to understand life as you become involved with people through your loving and caring personality. You should educate yourself and enhance your artistic abilities with poetry. Keep in check your acute psychic powers, as they can easily cloud your judgment. It is your purpose in life to find and experience new outlets in your endeavors.

Through new experiences you are able to introduce new concepts to others. It is your drive to establish your identity through individualism. You have an independent character and feel a need to be free from the interference of others. Although it conflicts with other sides of your nature, you are a practical person; you are also inventive in your ideas, creative with your hands, and original in your thought. You possess strong sexual desires. Your feelings supersede your actions. You love the outdoors and you find peace and tranquility in nature.

1 9 1 COMBINATION for: "MICHELE" or "DAN" or equivalent

You are candid; in conversations with others, you become argumentative. When given an opportunity, you get straight to the point. You can defend a person while sticking up for the opponent, as well. When aroused, you can be very sarcastic.

You lack verbal expression and lead a narrow life. You have few friends and crave affection. You like straight talk and are not secretive. You are not easily hurt and will call a spade a spade. You have a rough-and-ready type of personality.

Ironically, you are seen as a refined, religious personality, affectionate with the needy and holding no grudges.

2 1 3 COMBINATION for: "SANDRA" or "LEROY" or equivalent

You are a very diplomatic person. You possess creative talents in art, music, and singing. You have too many love affairs, and you can lie cheerfully and look innocent. You find it difficult to control your behavior, and you tend to be too easy-going.

You have a strong natural sense of harmony in all matters. You desire peace at any price. You are a daydreamer, and you can be temperamental when provoked. Your disposition is governed by emotions rather than by logic and reason; at times your emotions control your actions. You have problems concentrating, and you lack the ability to be systematic. You are not a practical person; you love to spend money, are fond of sugars and starchy foods, and you gossip too much. However, your quick thinking rescues you from imminent disaster.

To others, you are the picture of independence, self-reliance, and originality. You are happy and optimistic, and your compassion for people could bring them a great deal of inspiration.

You can maintain a positive disposition through constructive thought and action, keeping at bay negative beliefs about your personal performance. In business and in your personal life, you love to entertain and express yourself, but your active imagination can sometimes go overboard. You dress immaculately, like to show off on stage, and perform best in large crowds; in fact, you are always per-forming. Selling new, groundbreaking products excites you and your adaptability keeps you employed.

Your devotion to your loved ones is spontaneous and your outlook on life is cosmopolitan. Your pleasant demeanor can be laced with humor and you thrive upon kindness.

2 2 4 COMBINATION for: "JOYCE" or "CHRISTOPHER" or equivalent

There is no positive side to the qualities of this name. When called by this name you lack vision and inspiration. You are slow in picking up conversational meanings, your power of concentration is dwarfed, you do not pay attention, you get overly emotional, fussy over little things, and you lack confidence. You lack inspiration. You have a terrible time concentrating. You are absent-minded, over-emotional, and tend to cry over nothing.

If you'd like to make a change to your name, please read the information on Name Analysis in the last pages of this book.

2 3 5 COMBINATION for: "PATRICIA" or "LEO" or equivalent

You are very discordant; you have a dashing appearance, but with disappointment to follow. Having no depth of mind, you attract the wrong type of individuals, and this causes you bitter experiences. You are overly emotional and sometimes chaotic. You develop an unstable personality with no evolution or stability. Your personal affairs are in turmoil and you become witty but untruthful.

There is no positive side to this mathematical equivalent. If you'd like to make a change to your name, please read the information on Name Analysis in the last pages of this book.

2 4 6 COMBINATION for: "CONNIE" or "ROBERT" or equivalent

The adoption of this name made you a pleasant and easy-going person. Your visionary capabilities and the development of an excellent business mind, in combination with a practical and tactful personality, have made you loved by others. You are sympathetic and forgiving. You have a strong and lasting love for people close to you, so honest relationships are possible. To that special person close to your heart, you show love, devotion, affection, and forgiveness.

You love to take on responsibility for others and to care for their needs. Organization is your defining characteristic...you are able to organize your business and personal life in your sleep. You are gifted with the ability to balance the art of living. Nothing can deter you from getting what you want.

People can come to you to talk about general or personal problems; they always receive an abundance of useful information. Your social activities are numerous, and you are more than welcome to attend and lead social activities in your community. Your intelligence and trustworthiness are highly respected. Your quiet, stable personality is only superseded by your understanding and friendly disposition. You are responsible, honest, and inspirational to others. You have excellent taste. You are studious, mature, and like to do business independently.

This name combination does not possess negative or flip side vibration qualities. Other people see in you a technical person, a strong, stable, rugged personality and a steadfast, stable character to match.

2 5 7 COMBINATION for: "ELIZABETH" or "CLARENCE" or equivalent

You are a quiet and refined person, extremely sensitive and emotional. You are negative towards anything that opposes you. You are not aggressive, but your nervousness drains you of all your reserve strength. You are idealistic in your approach to things, jealous of others' success and easily hurt when bested. You can be moody without apparent reason. To others you appear calm when, in fact, you are nervous. This tends to cause a nervous condition in your solar plexus.

You have a natural gift for reflecting on your inner nature and you tend to seek the mysteries of life in the universe. You are quiet and it seems that you go about things deep in thought. You are a natural philosopher and love to dwell in the depths of religion. Your sensitivity is acute; you can sense things before they become realized. You can look at a person and know what he or she is about to say before they say it, and this makes others indifferent towards you; they think you are secretive and stuck up. You can sense a lot more than you may be able to express, causing you to retreat from normal activities while being misunderstood by others. Your idealism is surpassed by your studious, psychic personality and your natural, gentle ways. You should educate yourself about your emotional shortcomings.

You are refined and love the outdoors. Little things make you happy; a single flower can arouse deep appreciation while a bouquet of roses would leave you cold. You love nature and find peace and harmony among the trees, rolling hills, and blue skies. This name combination offers poor business sense and promotes a lack of responsibility. Physical weaknesses are evident in the heart, lung, and upper respiratory regions.

If you'd like to make a change to your name, please read the information on Name Analysis in the last pages of this book.

2 6 8 COMBINATION for: "CLARE" or "MOSES" or equivalent

You are a sophisticated person; you appreciate money and value. You are wise and diplomatic; you would make a good business executive. You are drawn into excellent financial positions. You enjoy expensive, quality goods. If your name is unbalanced, then to some degree the vibration denotes negative qualities; you can become, or are, a shrewd, calculating person who dislikes work, and you may try to marry into money. You lack self-confidence and are always on the look out for an easy dollar. You want to look nice, so you are willing to spend money on expensive clothing. For materialistic reasons, you are a loving and affectionate person, but you can go overboard. Your inner nature, however, is giving, and you like to share and help the needy.

The yearning for financial independence is predominant in your life and becomes realized at an early age through your personal independence, and you only accept positions in which you have power and control over commodities and decision-making. Your ambition helps you overcome obstacles with ease and your endless energy and stamina allows you to forge ahead to reach your goals. Your analytical mind causes you to quickly assume responsibility, and sometimes you take calculated risks when winning is in your favor. Your solutions are practical and versatile, your powerful nature is accumulative, and your independent character is charitable and honest.

You have to keep in check your negative emotions, which tend to cause you to over-exaggerate things and buy expensive commodities.

If you'd like to make a change to your name, please read the information on Name Analysis in the last pages of this book.

2 7 9 COMBINATION for: "MARCIA" or ROGER" or equivalent

You are a generous person, very nice and passive. You desire peace and harmony. Early in life you feel the need to search for truth and share your wisdom with the masses. You are an inspirational guide to many and your need to strive for perfection makes you an expert in your field. You leave the audience spellbound when you speak. Through your personal evolution you find the purpose in your life and in the lives of others. Your advanced inspirational talents should be shared with others.

Your deep religious feelings are clarified through evolution of self. You begin to understand life as you become involved with others through your loving and caring personality. Your sensitivity demonstrates your compassion for others and your generosity alleviates suffering. You do not hold grudges and you are affectionate.

You should educate yourself and enhance your artistic abilities with poetry. Keep in check your acute psychic powers, as they can easily cloud your judgment.

2 8 1 COMBINATION for: "REBECCA" or "ADAM" or equivalent

This combination has a negative and discordant vibration, with little to offer. If your name has the mathematical equivalent of 281, you are friendly until things go against you. You are a slow thinker, without deep reasoning power, so you have a difficult time learning. Your mental capacity is limited. If approached in the wrong way, you can become belligerent.

There is no positive side to the above names. If you'd like to make a change to your name, please read the information on Name Analysis in the last pages of this book.

2 9 2 COMBINATION for: "DIANA" or CARTER" or equivalent

The qualities of your name oppose your true qualities (the real you). You like to sit behind the television with a snack while the real you wants action. You are in constant conflict, though you cannot bear turmoil and will make peace under any circumstances. Your agreeable nature is appealing to others and you are able to make friends in high places. Your lively, conversational, and sometimes witty expressions draw friendly gestures and laughter. You are tactful, courteous, and pleasant.

You have extraordinary abilities in art, music, drama, politics, catering, hospital care, and selling merchandise. You are a dreamer and you can tell a beautiful story with a pleasant and warmhearted sincerity that leaves others spellbound. You are a natural peacemaker, generous to others though easily led, and you are fond of pleasure and relaxation. You are a sweet person and the opposite sex receives a good deal of romantic attention from you.

Your name is not balanced, so you draw negative impulses from it: you hate to be alone, you are overly passive, overly sensitive, and you love to gossip. You are weak and you have problems making decisions; you'd rather take it easy and let others handle difficult problems. Because of a lack of determination, you sometimes need encouragement to get you through the day. Your office is disorganized, you have trouble concentrating, and you hate to budget. Your lack of confidence in yourself causes you to lose business opportunities. You dislike leadership.

However, you are an extremely sociable person and you like to teach and work with others; you would do well as a salesperson, diplomat, secretary, teacher, social worker, or in any occupation that allows you to work closely with people.

There is no positive side to the above names. If you'd like to make a change to your name, please read the information on Name Analysis in the last pages of this book.

3 1 4 COMBINATION for: "RUTH" or "RUSTY" or equivalent

Although you offer inspiration to others and you'd like to display your creative talents, you are limited in this by the mechanical and technical aspects of your makeup. Your creative and technical sides compete, and it will be difficult to determine which survives. Nevertheless, you have a strong natural sense of harmony in all matters.

Your devotion to your loved ones is spontaneous and your outlook on life is cosmopolitan. You have the potential to be a homebody and your cooking is second to none. Your pleasant demeanor can be laced with humor and you thrive upon kindness. Your compassion is inspiring and you are happy and optimistic. You can maintain this positive disposition through constructive thought and action, keeping at bay negative beliefs about your personal performance.

In business and in your personal life, you love to entertain and express yourself. You dress nicely. Selling new, groundbreaking products excites you, and your adaptable character keeps you employed. However, you can also be skeptical, demanding scientific proof before you accept something as fact. You count the pennies when given change. When others fail while performing monotonous tasks, you are just beginning. You love tedious projects and your patient, steady efforts always win in the end. Your analytical ability helps you access nature's innermost secrets, but you lose sight of the overall picture easily, so you should concentrate on concept. You excel at work in which you can deal with the details of an operation and/or numerical perfection.

You have a strong, stable, rugged personality and a stead-fast character to match. You are trustworthy, deliberate in your planning, and firm in your decisions.

You are thorough, neat, steady, and pragmatic; you are also punctual, patient, and technical.

3 2 5 COMBINATION for: "CAROLINE" or "RUDY" or equivalent

You are a creative and versatile person with numerous artistic talents. You speak well and can discuss a variety of subjects. You are friendly and dashing and your appearance exhibits good taste. You feel a lot more than you express; sometimes this is bad, if you do not control your impulsive reactions. You are an inspirational person; you are also constructive, intuitive, dynamic, and sometimes witty.

However, you are a restless person, not wanting to settle down. Your inner need for change and travel is almost unbearable; you are in constant need of change. You start many things you have problems finishing; you start with great interest but quickly lose it if the project becomes too monotonous or detailed. Your lack of stability can cause you to become involved in undesirable matters through the influence of others. You have problems saving money and are fond of the opposite sex.

Your desire to understand the forces of nature is awakened early in life. You desire freedom and the ability to think without the interference of others, but you must control the tendency to be intolerant, critical, and impatient. You would make a great traveling salesperson or aviator. You would also excel in work that allows you freedom of thought and action and in which you can promote new ideas and/or products.

3 3 6 COMBINATION for: "DOROTHY" or "LEONARD" or equivalent

This name is well balanced. It suits the make-up of the individual qualities of your inner self. This name is aligned with the vibrations of nature in the physical universe, and so it is in harmony with other life forms. With this name, you are a sunny, happy person with inspirational and practical aspects that allow you to be in touch with others who have the same qualities.

You are very expressive, but you are also reliable and stable. You are able to concentrate on and finish tasks, and your organizational abilities help you to be resourceful and efficient. Your emotions are well balanced and you are unable to speak an unkind word. You love to be appreciated. You are open-minded and a good listener. Because of this, you are able to dwell in the obvious as well as the abstract. You are a responsible person; you never allow bills to remain unpaid. You see education as mandatory for success in life and allow your children to have the best schools you can afford. You follow through with your plans with great determination and reach your goals triumphantly. Your sense of responsibility extends into other areas: you are a respected member of your community; you attend meetings, and you are punctual. Others can bet upon your dependability and trust your word.

You possess a healthy mind, as well as a healthy appetite. If your eating habits could be curtailed, you would spend most of your life away from hospitals and doctors' offices.

3 4 7 COMBINATION for: "LUCY" or "BURT" or equivalent

You are empathetic, even hypersensitive, and able to read others' thoughts; however, this makes you self-conscious and so you remain silent. You are quiet and it seems that you go about things deep in thought. You can sense a lot more than you may be able to express, causing you to retreat from normal activities while being misunderstood by others. You can sense things before they happen; you can look at people and know what they will say before they say it, and this makes others indifferent towards you, since they think you are secretive and stuck up. Generally, you are not very talkative because you see the ignorance and selfishness of those around you.

You are very lonely and you crave love and affection. You daydream and worry a lot. There are times when you feel overwhelmed by uncontrollable thoughts and feelings. You have a natural gift for expressing your inner nature and seeking the mysteries of life in the universe. You are a born philosopher and love to dwell in the depths of religion.

You are a refined person, and not being understood is the greatest disappointment in your life, contributing to your emotional instability. You best express your thoughts with the pen. You excel in composition and are an excellent writer. You also have other, numerous artistic talents. You inspire dormant personalities. You are very clever and not many people can get the better of you.

You love nature and the outdoors, and you need peace and tranquility, which you find among the trees, rolling hills, and blue skies. Little things make you happy; a single flower (rose) would bring you greater pleasure than a bouquet. Your idealism is surpassed only by your studious, psychic personality and your natural, gentle ways. You should educate yourself about your emotional shortcomings.

3 5 8 COMBINATION for: "DEBORAH" or "GUY" or equivalent

Others judge you by how you appear to them. They see in you a person who can't sit still, is always on the move, and scattered; you have too many things going at the same time. You are able to organize a business or your private life without training. The yearning for financial independence is predominant in your life and becomes realized at an early age through your personal independence. Thus, you only accept positions in which you have power and control over commodities and decision-making. Your ambition helps you to overcome obstacles with ease and your endless energy and stamina allow you to forge ahead to reach your goals.

In business and in your personal life, you love to entertain and express yourself. Selling new, groundbreaking products excites you. You dress immaculately, like to show off on stage, and perform best in large crowds. Your quick thinking tends to rescue you from imminent disaster. You have a very active imagination and can go overboard.

You have an analytical mind and you quickly assume responsibility; sometimes you take calculated risks when winning is in your favor. Your solutions are practical and versatile, your powerful nature is accumulative, and your character is charitable and honest. You have to keep in check your negative emotions, which tend to over-exaggerate things and make you buy expensive commodities. However, your adaptability keeps you employed.

Your inner nature is giving; you like to share and help the needy. You have a desire to inspire others, show off your lifestyle, and display your natural talents. You have a strong natural sense of harmony in all matters. Your devotion to your loved ones is spontaneous and your outlook on life is cosmopolitan. Your pleasant demeanor can be laced with humor and you thrive upon kindness. Your compassion for people brings them a great deal of inspiration. You are happy and optimistic.

You can maintain this positive disposition through constructive thought and action, keeping at bay negative beliefs about your personal performance.

3 6 9 COMBINATION for: "JUDITH" or CURTIS" or equivalent

The above names and/or mathematical equivalent of 369 is better for a woman than a man, as it destroys some masculinity. It does enhance music and artistic abilities and creates a spontaneous and generous nature. You are very lovable. You are dramatic; you like to demonstrate your feelings and can put on an act that would put a professional to shame. You are an excellent dancer and have a gift for music. You have a desire to help others, are deeply religious, and are highly impressionable.

You love to "show off," no matter what you're doing. You dress nicely, demonstrate your accomplishments, and express yourself in many other ways. You are imaginative in thought and action and expressive and highly emotional, especially in love-related situations. You do not hold grudges and you are affectionate with the needy; in fact, your affectionate nature is overwhelming.

Through your personal evolution you find your purpose in life. Your sensitivity demonstrates your compassion for others and your generosity alleviates suffering. Your deep religious feelings receive clarity through evolution of self. You begin to understand life as you become involved with others through your loving and caring personality.

Your inspirational inner nature is a natural endowment you are to share with others. Early in life, you recognize the need to search for the truth and the desire to share this wisdom with the masses. You are an inspirational guide to many and your need to strive for perfection makes you the expert in your field. You leave an audience spellbound when you speak.

You should educate yourself and enhance your artistic abilities with poetry. Keep in check your acute psychic powers, as they easily can cloud your judgment.

3 7 1 COMBINATION for: "LORETTA" or "GORDON" or equivalent

This name is totally destructive. You are severely negative, unproductive and unbalanced with regard to your inner nature. The vibration of this name generally makes you intolerant, candid when provoked, sarcastic when opposed, and domineering over all issues and situations. You are straight to the point and determined to get your way. You can be argumentative and unfriendly, and you lack reasoning abilities. You express yourself in a negative and offensive manner. Your conversation is self-centered. You are generally unreasonable.

There is no positive side to the above names and/or mathematical equivalent. If you'd like to make a change to your name, please read the information on Name Analysis in the last pages of this book.

3 8 2 COMBINATION for: "LEONA" or "BUDDY" or equivalent

Your name expresses some of the finer qualities of your inner self but also indicates qualities not belonging to you through birth, thereby creating a separate entity not in accordance with your mental and physical makeup. This causes discord; therefore, you will find some of your behavior relevant and understandable and other parts of your behavior patterns alien to you.

Through your first name, you are a good-natured, sympathetic individual whose loving nature is adored by all who have the pleasure of your company. Your friendly personality is only surpassed by your idealism, and your likable nature makes you desired by others, sometimes more than you can bear. Your peacekeeping abilities keep in check both children and adults. Often you are too easy-going and become overly emotional about the problems of others. You have some musical and artistic talents, and you can easily lose yourself to daydreaming and then have problems concentrating.

You do not like to hurt the feelings of others and so stretch the truth in conversations. With this name, it is impossible to accumulate, and you are led to over-indulge.

3 9 3 COMBINATION for: "RUBY" or "JUSTIN" or equivalent

You are happy, spontaneous, generous, expressive, bubbly, and full of fun. You love to meet and mix with others. Your devotion to your loved ones is spontaneous and your outlook is cosmopolitan. Your pleasant demeanor can be laced with humor and you thrive upon kindness. You are extremely generous and sympathetic, and you love to talk and be the center of attention. Love is your motivating force, and your compassion for people can bring them a great deal of inspiration. You are spontaneous and imaginative, gifted in arts and drama. You have a strong natural sense of harmony in all matters. You should educate yourself to be more systematic, using your natural talents in a more orderly fashion.

In business and in your personal life, you love to entertain and express yourself. Selling new, groundbreaking products excites you, and your adaptability keeps you employed. You dress immaculately, like to show off on stage, and perform best in large crowds; in one way or another, you are always performing. Your have an active imaginative, which can sometimes go overboard.

You are happy and optimistic in outlook. You can maintain this positive disposition through constructive thought and action, keeping at bay negative beliefs about your personal performance. Your quick thinking rescues you from imminent disaster.

4 1 5 COMBINATION for: "GEORGIANA" or "ARTHUR" or equivalent

You are constructive in your efforts, intuitive, dynamic, and sometimes witty, but the above names and/or mathematical equivalent 415 are detrimental to your inner self. Your name interferes with your personality, character, and your type of nature. It prevents you from performing and forces you to adopt qualities contrary to your makeup. The sooner you disown this name the better off you will be in health, success, and spiritual equilibrium. This name is very unstable.

There are two opposing forces working against one another. On the one hand, you desire system and concentration, making progress one-step at a time. On the other hand, you are constantly forced into new experiences that cause instability and change.

This name causes repression and turmoil. You desire to test things, to strive for numerical perfection, and you would like to be strong, rugged, deliberate, thorough, and steadfast. However, while others see you as an active person, self-confident, candid, intellectually powerful, inventive, and authoritative, in reality this name forces constant upheaval, causing you to continue to change your environment and your work.

You undergo geographical relocation in an attempt to experience a new life, and you seek adventure, but this only contributes to your difficulties; the development of physical disorders and an unsettled spirit. You find it difficult to complete things; you start with great interest but quickly lose it if the project becomes too monotonous or detailed. Early in life you recognize a desire to find the reasons behind the forces of nature. You must control your intolerance, criticism, and impatience. You desire freedom of thought and would make a great traveling salesperson or aviator. You would also excel in work that allows you freedom of thought and action, in which you can promote new ideas and/or products.

4 2 6 COMBINATION for: "AUDRY" or "MURRAY" or equivalent

You are a technical individual; you tend to assume responsibility; you have a constructive disposition and great depth of thought. You desire quality and are very appreciative and philosophical. You are patient, like people, and are a great homemaker. You are stable and tend not to like to stray.

Organization is one of your strengths. You are able to organize your business and personal life in your sleep. People can consult with you about general or personal problems and always receive an abundance of useful information.

You are gifted with the ability to balance the art of living. Your social activities are numerous and you are more than welcome to attend and lead social activities in your community. Your intelligence and trustworthiness are highly respected. Your quiet, stable personality is only superseded by your understanding and friendly disposition. You are responsible, honest, and inspirational to others. You have excellent taste. You are studious, mature, and you like to do business independently. You are accumulative and nothing can deter you from getting what you want, but you are willing to take responsibility for your actions. People can rely on your judgment and depend on your promises.

4 3 7 COMBINATION for: "AVALONE" or "ORLANDO" or equivalent

With the above names, you are constantly in conflict with others. You are destructive, highly emotional, with a distinctly chaotic nature. You have problems controlling your appetite, lack verbal expression, and have very little or no ability to accumulate. You are mostly misunderstood, and you misunderstand others frequently. You are plagued with loneliness.

Over time, you develop an acute, sensitive nature: you can sense what others are about to say before they say it, but this makes others indifferent toward you; they think you are secretive and stuck-up.

There is no positive side to the above names and/or mathematical equivalent. If you'd like to make a change to your name, please read the information on Name Analysis in the last pages of this book.

4 4 8 COMBINATION for: "JULIA" or "APPOLO" or equivalent

You are very responsible, extremely practical, and tend to be masculine. You are cautious in your endeavors, systematic, and sensible. You are skeptical and demand scientific proof before you accept something as fact. You count the pennies when given change. When others fail while performing monotonous tasks, you are just beginning. You love tedious projects and your patient, slow, and steady efforts always win in the end. Your analytical ability helps you access nature's innermost secrets.

However, you lose sight of the big picture easily, so you should concentrate on concept. You excel in work in which you can deal with the details of an operation and/or numerical perfection. You have a strong, stable, rugged personality and a steadfast, stable character to match. You have the potential to be a homebody and your cooking is second to none. You are trustworthy, deliberate in your planning, and firm in your decisions. You are thorough, neat, and steady, and you are punctual, patient, pragmatic, and technical. You are able to organize a business or your private life without training.

The yearning for financial independence is predominant in your life and becomes realized at an early age through personal independence. Thus you only accept positions in which you have power and control over commodities and decision-making.

Your inner nature is giving; you like to share and help the needy. Your ambition allows you to overcome obstacles with ease and your endless energy and stamina help you forge ahead to reach your goals. You tend to assume responsibility and sometimes take calculated risks when winning is in your favor. Your solutions are practical and versatile, your powerful nature is accumulative, and your character is charitable and honest. You have to keep in check your negative emotions, which tend to over-exaggerate things and make you buy expensive commodities.

4 5 9 COMBINATION for: "ROSAMOND" or "STUART" or equivalent

Under the above names, you develop frustration and lack expression. You are scattered and unsympathetic. Your uncontrollable temper is only superseded by your powerful sexual urges.

There is no positive side to the above names and/or mathematical equivalent. If you'd like to make a change to your name, please read the information on Name Analysis in the last pages of this book.

4 6 1 COMBINATION for: "CLEOPATRA" or "ALFONSO" or equivalent

You are a hard worker and choose your endeavors along the lines of pioneering. You have the desire to educate yourself about the technical and mechanical side of life. If your name has been with you from birth, you are a born engineer. You are skeptical and demand scientific proof before you accept something as fact. You count the pennies when given change. You have the potential to be a homebody and your cooking is second to none. When others fail while performing monotonous tasks, you are just beginning. You love tedious projects and your patient and steady efforts always win in the end. You excel in work in which you can deal with the details of an operation and/or numerical perfection. Your analytical abilities allow you to access nature's innermost secrets. However, you lose sight of the big picture easily, so you should concentrate on concept.

You have a strong, stable, rugged personality and a steadfast, stable character to match. You are trustworthy, deliberate in your planning, and firm in your decisions. You are thorough, neat, and steady, punctual, patient, and technical. You are a practical person, inventive in your ideas, creative with your hands, and original in your thought. Your feelings can supersede your action. You possess strong sexual desires, and you can be blunt when aroused and sarcastic when provoked. You love the outdoors and find peace and tranquility in nature. You love to challenge your physical strength with the forces of nature. In business, your success lies in the practical aspect of things. You are a born leader and you work best in an environment in which your perseverance, self-reliance, and leadership qualities can be introduced.

4 7 2 COMBINATION for: "SUSAN" or "HUBBARD" or equivalent

People see in you a natural philosopher who loves to dwell in the depths of religion, is indifferent towards others, and secretive and stuck up. In reality, you are helping to bring people together to create peace and harmony. It is your duty to examine the mind and soul of others. You are tolerant, tactful, and diplomatic. You are a sensitive, refined person who opposes turmoil and hardship of any kind. You like to be involved in curing human suffering, which you cannot bear to witness personally.

Witnessing atrocities committed on others brings you great agony. You need to learn to be more active mentally and physically, because too often you have the tendency to take it easy. Your natural craving for peace and happiness is expressed in the slow pace with which you like to set things in motion. Learn to confront adversities and be decisive in your actions. Get involved in decision-making with others through the diplomacy so natural to you. Become involved in the problems of others to find success and happiness.

4 8 3 COMBINATION for: "JULIETTE" or "MARCUS" or equivalent

You have a great imagination, are creative, good-natured, and you love to excel. People think you are a great organizer, financially independent, and a powerful decision-maker. You are inspirational and have a strong sense of harmony. Your compassion can bring people a great deal of inspiration. You are happy and optimistic. You can maintain this positive disposition through constructive thought and action, keeping at bay negative beliefs about your personal performance.

In business and in your personal life, you love to entertain and express yourself. Selling new, groundbreaking products gives you excitement. You dress immaculately, like to show off on stage, and perform best in large crowds; in fact, you're always performing. Your imagination is sometimes too active, but your quick thinking rescues you from imminent disaster.

Your devotion to your loved ones is spontaneous and your outlook on life is cosmopolitan. Your adaptability keeps you employed. Your pleasant demeanor can be laced with humor and you thrive upon kindness.

4 9 4 COMBINATION for: "MUREEN" or "DONOVAN" or equivalent

You are systematic, a scheduler. You have great mathematical abilities and unshakable patience and concentration. When you start a project, you are determined to see it through to the end. You are deliberate and direct. You constantly strive to be better. You have a scientific mind and spend a great deal of time researching ways to improve your business. The rewards of this are evident in your spending weakness.

You are obsessed by accuracy. You have a problem tolerating the lesser-gifted person. You love to work alone and are good at it. You start when others give up, especially at tedious projects. Your slow but precise drive always gets you to reach your goals. You are a stickler for details. Example: When someone short-changes you, you will count say, "You are short one cent" and then follow up with, "How do you plan to pay it?"

Your office, workplace and home are immaculate. You always allow enough time to have room for eventualities. You are good with your hands and you can produce greatly detailed product samples.

Physically, you develop a robust body.

5 1 6 COMBINATION for: "SHIRLEY" or "FRED" or equivalent

You are a very active, intense person, original in your ideas and independent in every facet of your make-up. You develop a stable and responsible character. Your mind is capable of deep, complex thinking, giving you vision and foresight. People with this name vibration make excellent managers, as they have principled natures and authoritative dispositions. You do not tolerate interference from others, and you work best when you are able to make your own plans and carry them out. You are studious, mature, and you have excellent taste. You are accumulative and tend to take responsibility for your actions. People can rely on your judgment and depend on your promises. Your intelligence and trustworthiness are highly respected.

To others you look like a hard worker, independent, with strong emotions, sure of yourself.

Gifted with the ability to balance the art of living, you are adept at organizing your business and personal life. People can consult with you about general or personal problems and always receive an abundance of useful information. Your social activities are numerous and you are more than welcome to attend and lead social activities in your community.

Nothing can deter you from getting what you want. You have a quiet, stable personality and an understanding and friendly disposition. You are responsible, honest, and inspirational to others.

5 2 7 COMBINATION for: "LYNNE" or "HENRY" or equivalent

Your numerous fine qualities are imprisoned by the negative vibrations of your name and are causing tremendous stress on your mind and body. Your intuitive nature is overworked, making you overly sensitive and resulting in restless, sleepless nights. You are self-conscious of your sensitivity toward others because you are often misinterpreted, causing you to shut down completely. You speak what your name dictates rather than what you desire, making you frustrated, at best. Your artistic abilities are repressed by your unwanted business activities. You have a keen mind and think deeply, but since this happens at the most inopportune times, people presume you are daydreaming or spaced out. This is very frustrating to you and causes you to retreat from the company of others.

You express yourself through writing. The ideal place for you is away from people and close to nature. You enjoy and appreciate the finer things in life and you dress nicely. You convey yourself vividly through art. The little things thrill you most; a single red rose would do miracles for you while a large bouquet leaves you cold. You do well playing outdoor sports. For health reasons, it is very important you spend a great deal of time outdoors and close to nature.

Only nature can fill your needs and bring you peace and tranquility. Because of the imbalance of your name, you are high strung and intense. You are able to sense invisible forces around you, and your intuitive powers play a large role in predicting forthcoming events. Contrary to your inner nature, you at times lack verbal expression. You try to make friends to reduce your lonely existence, yet a great deal of the time you want to be alone, something no one else understands.

5 3 8 COMBINATION for: "LAURA" or "ERIC" or equivalent

You desire independence and self-sufficiency. Your ambition is only surpassed by your excellent business judgment, which makes you generally and financially accumulative. Your sense of quality gives you the edge over competitors in the sales arena, and gives you the opportunity to establish a comfortable home. You must refrain from the urge to gamble, as well as to assume too many financial responsibilities. Some of the following desires are lurking under the surface and are felt under the name, though they may not necessarily be realized: a new work environment, a change in lifestyle, and a change in location. Your need for accuracy or exactness in your dealings with others is somewhat realized. You desire freedom from all limitations.

Your original and versatile ideas find fertile ground, especially in the business world, where your creativity finds an effective outlet in the promotional field. You have a sharp and analytical mind, which is enhanced and fully supported by your inner nature, so you are able to realize great achievements. Your charitable desires are repressed by the necessity to keep your independence. Your changeable but ambitious drive should be curtailed; you should learn to relax and balance your activities. You market your creativity with a logical approach.

You work best alone and unrestricted. You seek truth, fact, and logic in the general sense, and you love nature and outdoor occupations. You dislike monotony and seek the mental companionship of older people. You must avoid overindulgence and control unstable moods. Relax when things get too stressed out to control your candid tongue or quick temper. According to the evaluation of this name, you must be careful not to become unsociable, unsystematic, contemptuous, and self-destructive.

Physical setbacks are in the generative areas. Also, check your body for tumors.

5 4 9 COMBINATION for: "BETTY" or "RITCHIE" or equivalent

You desire to help humanity. You appreciate the deeper things in life. You are a great reformer and you constantly want to improve. You are not accumulative, are radical in your thoughts, and you hate repression. Often you are depressed and moody. There is a lot of tension at home and you suffer from nervous conditions. You are quick-tempered.

Through your personal evolution you find the purpose in your life and in the lives of others. Your sensitivity demonstrates your compassion for others and your generosity alleviates their suffering. Early in life you recognize the need to search for the truth and the desire to share this wisdom with the masses. You are an inspirational guide to many and your need to strive for perfection makes you the expert in your field. You leave the audience spellbound when you speak. It is your purpose in life to inspire others and guide them onto the path leading to their spiritual inheritance. You are to share your wisdom and inspiration with others.

You do not hold grudges and you are affectionate with the needy. Your deep religious feelings receive clarity through evolution of self. You begin to understand life as you become involved with others. You should educate yourself and enhance your artistic abilities with poetry. Keep in check your acute psychic powers as they can easily cloud your judgment.

Your physical weaknesses are in the central nervous system.

5 5 1 COMBINATION for: "BECKY" or "KELVIN" or equivalent

The above names can have devastating effects on your equilibrium; your name is preventing you from realizing the potential inner self given to you through birth. Your ability to express your inner self was taken away, and to some extent, the name suppressed the qualities of your inner self. The longer this name works upon you the worse the conditions become. This name demands you abide by its qualities even if contrary to your will. You find changes in yourself, not because you grew older, but because you developed the unsuitable qualities in your name. With this name you have developed a turbulent and candid disposition, strong sexual desires and intense depression. You have become increasingly argumentative and hard to get along with.

You love the outdoors and you find peace and tranquility in nature. You love to challenge your physical strength with the forces of nature. You are a practical person, inventive and creative with your hands. In business, your success lies in the practical aspect of things. You are a born leader and you work best in an environment in which your perseverance, self-reliance and leadership qualities can be introduced. Your feelings supersede your actions; you can be blunt when aroused and sarcastic when provoked.

This name affects your nervous system, causes headaches, female problems, sets the stage for major operations, and induces accidents.

5 6 2 COMBINATION for: "KITTIE" or "MIKE" or equivalent

You have a sense of refinement, which is expressed in tolerance, and with this understanding you bring tact and diplomacy to others. By nature, you are a sensitive, refined person who opposes turmoil and hardship of any kind. You like to be involved with the remedying of human suffering, which you cannot bear to witness personally; witnessing atrocities committed on others brings you tremendous agony.

If this combination is a nickname, you developed into a different person, with fewer advantages than the names described above. Your imagination, likable personality, and sales abilities were intensified. But at times your activities were stunted by your inability to function properly. You listened to people who could not advise you, shied away from responsibility, became impulsive and over-indulgent, and your temperament flared up frequently.

You need to educate yourself to be more active with your mind and body. Too often you have the tendency to want to take it easy. Your natural craving for peace and happiness is the source for the slow pace with which you like to set things in motion. Learn to confront adversities and be decisive in your actions. Get involved in decision-making with others through the diplomacy so natural to you. Become involved in the problems of others to find success and happiness. In business, you could do very well working with the public.

5 7 3 COMBINATION for: "MYRTLE" or "KEN" or equivalent

You have a keen sense of truth and logic and an inner urge for change and travel, but you are able to control your impulses. You desire freedom of thought and have a strong sense of harmony in all matters; your desire to understand the forces of nature is awakened early in life. Your compassion for people could bring them a great deal of inspiration. You are happy and optimistic. You can maintain this positive disposition through constructive thought and action, keeping at bay negative beliefs about your personal performance.

In business and in your personal life, you love to entertain and express yourself. Selling new, ground-breaking products excites you. You dress immaculately, like to show off on stage, and you perform best in large crowds; in fact, you are always performing. You have an active imagination, which can go overboard. Your devotion to your loved ones is spontaneous and your outlook on life is cosmopolitan. Your adaptability keeps you employed. Your quick thinking rescues you from imminent disaster, but you must work to control your intolerance, criticism, and impatience. If you'd like to make a change to your name, please read the information on Name Analysis in the last pages of this book.

5 8 4 COMBINATION for: "BELL" or "JERRY" or equivalent

While you are mechanically inventive, you are also discordant. You have narrow vision, dislike monotony, have a strong sex drive, and are overly emotional. You have limited opportunities.

When others fail while performing monotonous tasks, you are just beginning. You love tedious projects and your patient and steady efforts always win in the end. Your analytical ability helps you access nature's innermost secrets.

You lose sight of the overall picture easily, thus you should concentrate on concept. You excel in work that allows you to deal with the details of an operation and/or numerical perfection. You have a strong, stable, rugged personality and a steadfast, stable character to match. You have the potential to be a homebody and your cooking is second to none. You are trustworthy in your actions, deliberate in your planning, and firm in your decisions. You are thorough, neat, steady, pragmatic, punctual, patient, and technical.

5 9 5 COMBINATION for: "JENNY" or "LEWIS" or equivalent

You are very intense and high-strung. You cannot stand to be belittled, and you become moody and depressed to a point at which you consider suicide. You are afraid of the things you might do to others when you lose your temper. Your emotions overwhelm your reasoning. You will do anything to dare opposition. This name makes you do what you say you will do, good or bad. You cannot stand to be taunted, and you could kill over it. You have a hard time relaxing and you carry on until you are exhausted. You have no peace of mind. Little things upset you and you make a mountain out of a molehill. It starts slowly and builds until you lose your temper, then the process starts all over again.

You always have obstacles to overcome. You have a clever, quick mind, but you do not get anywhere…your turbulent nature destroys every opportunity. You must be a major player in any game. You do not allow defeat, will not be made fun of, and cannot take adversity of any kind. You have difficulties finishing what you start, and you are accident-prone.

This name affects your solar plexus and your stomach. You are too high strung and you suffer breakdowns and depression.

6 1 7 COMBINATION for: "GRACE" or "WALKER" or equivalent

You like to counsel people about general or personal problems. They always receive an abundance of useful information. Your quiet, stable personality is only surpassed by your understanding and friendly disposition. You have a natural gift for reflection and seek out the mysteries of life in the universe. You are a natural philosopher and love to dwell in the depths of religion. Your sensitivity is acute. You can sense things before they become realized. You can look at a person and know what he or she is about to say before they say it, and this makes others indifferent towards you; they think you are secretive and stuck up. You are quiet and it seems that you go about things deep in thought. You can sense a lot more than you may be able to express, causing you to retreat from normal activities while being misunderstood by others. Your idealistic nature is surpassed by your studious, psychic personality and your natural, gentle ways.

You are refined and love the outdoors, finding peace and harmony among the trees, rolling hills, and blue skies. Little things make you happy. A single flower can arouse deep appreciation while a bouquet of roses would leave you cold. You are gifted with the ability to balance the art of living and nothing can deter you from getting what you want; however, you should educate yourself about your emotional shortcomings.

6 2 8 COMBINATION for: "BRENDA" or "ALLAN" or equivalent

This is a healthy and robust combination. If your undesired eating habits could be curtailed you would spend most of your life away from hospitals and doctors' offices. Your emotions are well balanced and you would never render an unkind word. People with this numerical combination possess a healthy mind.

You are open-minded and a good listener. You dwell in the obvious as well as the abstract. Your exceptionally good business judgment leads you to engage in any worthwhile business venture and you are especially successful if you have the knowledge of the Cyclic Law and the ability to activate its power. You are a responsible person who never allows bills to remain unpaid. You see education as mandatory for success in life and send your children to the best schools, with only cost as a limitation. You follow through with your plans with great determination and you reach your goals. Your responsibility extends to other areas, as well: you are a respected member of your community; you show up at meetings and arrive on time. Others can bet on you to keep your word.

You are a gifted organizer and a good leader, liked by many, particularly managers in the workplace. You know how to relax and recharge your energy. Your strong and stable character is envied by most. Your physical setbacks are evident only with an imbalance of your names. After registering your new name, you will slowly become the qualities of the new vibration, and you will be able to express the desires, personalities and character of your inner nature.

6 3 9 COMBINATION for: "SHEILA" or "EARL" or equivalent

You are intelligent, with a broad and complex mind. Your inner urge is to uplift others and make them feel happy. You assume too much responsibility, leaving you short when it comes to your own wants and needs. You do not hold grudges and you possess a very idealistic character, but your personal generosity must be curbed for your own welfare.

You are very creative and artistic. You can play musical instruments and love to listen to your favorite tunes, which give you a sense of peace and ease.

Early in life you recognize the need to search for truth and the desire to share this wisdom with the masses. You are an inspirational guide to many and your need to strive for perfection makes you the expert in your field. You leave the audience spellbound when you speak. Through your personal evolution you find the purpose in your life and in the lives of others. It is your purpose in life to inspire others through the knowledge of the universal wisdom and guide them onto the path leading to their spiritual inheritance. Your sensitivity demonstrates your compassion for others and your generosity alleviates their suffering.

You are affectionate with the needy, and your deep religious feelings receive clarity through evolution of self. You begin to understand life as you become involved with others.

You should control your worry over others and take additional time to relax, or tension will become a major ob-
stacle of good health. You should educate yourself and
enhance your artistic abilities with poetry. Keep in check
your acute psychic powers, as they easily can cloud your
judgment.

6 4 1 COMBINATION for: "FAYE" or "EDWARD" or equivalent

You are positive in your thoughts and decision-making and creative in your business approach. You are independent in your personal and business affairs, and that can be the reason why you do not want to marry. Pioneering gives you a chill of excitement. You love the outdoors and you find peace and tranquility in nature. You love to challenge your physical strength with the forces of nature.

Early in your life, you become aware of your independent character and the need to be free from the interference of others. Dwell in new experiences and introduce your new concepts to others. It is your duty to establish your identity through individualism.

You possess strong sexual desires and your feelings supersede your actions . . . you can be blunt when aroused and sarcastic when provoked. But you are a very honest person, and your generally good nature is appreciated and increases your self-assurance.

Basically, you are a practical person, inventive in your ideas, creative with your hands, and original in thought. In business, your success lies in the practical aspect of things. You are a born leader and you work best in an environment in which your perseverance, self-reliance, and leadership qualities can be introduced.

6 5 2 COMBINATION for: "RACHEL" or "JOHN" or equivalent

You are intellectually gifted, reliable, responsible, and home loving. You are self-reliant and desire a stable, well-rounded, accumulative life: you wish to settle down, assume responsibilities, and handle commodities. You are conscientious and like to direct the efforts of others, particularly in large groups.

You are generally cheerful and modest, but you have very definite opinions. At times, you are bossy, opinionated, fussy, and self-centered. You worry a lot and lack concentration. You are inclined to be too domineering and superior in your attitudes, but you can also be tactful and diplomatic. You always look restful to others. Your good judgment makes you successful, and everyone appreciates your honesty. Your kindness and even temper create harmony among loved ones.

You are a non-aggressive, peaceful person, and you appreciate art, music, and literature. By nature, you are sensitive and refined, opposing turmoil and hardship of any kind. You like to be involved in the remedying of human suffering, which you cannot bear to witness personally. Witnessing atrocities committed on others causes you tremendous agony.

You need to educate yourself to be more active with your mind and body, because, too often, you have the tendency to want to it take it easy. Your natural craving for peace and happiness is the source for the slow pace with which you like to set things in motion. Learn to confront adversities and be decisive in your actions. Get involved in decision-making with others using your diplomatic talents. Become involved in the problems of others to find success and happiness. In business, you could do very well working with the public.

6 6 3 COMBINATION for: "DEBRA" or "JAMES" or equivalent

You are an intellectual individual with a cheerful personality. You are patient and modest, responsible and reliable. Your home is your castle and you are conscientious and accumulative. You have very definite opinions, are self-reliant, and desire a stable, well rounded, and accumulative life. You desire to settle down and assume business responsibilities, handle commodities, and employ others. You are thrifty and have an appreciation of art, music, and literature.

You love home and children and desire to marry early. You yearn to settle down so you can stabilize your efforts. You wish to direct the efforts of others, particularly in large groups, and you are an excellent business manager, clever and quick thinking.

People love to work for you. You are a natural entertainer, socially inclined and companionable. You search for a position that allows you to express yourself creatively. You are romantic, emotional, spontaneous, and affectionate. You are sympathetic towards others and are always pleasant. You are trustworthy, a good business executive with a generous heart.

6 7 4 COMBINATION for: "KAREN" or "ROY" or equivalent

You are practical and systematic in your plans and actions. You are a patient organizer, stable and accumulative. Your responsibilities are met with trustworthiness and honesty. Your hard work is successful through your endurance and precise planning.

You have a strong, stable, rugged personality and a steadfast, stable character to match. You have the potential to be a homebody and your cooking is second to none.

You are skeptical and demand scientific proof before you accept something as fact. You count the pennies when given change. When others fail while performing monotonous tasks, you are just beginning. You love tedious projects and your patient and steady efforts always win in the end. Your analytical ability helps you access nature's innermost secrets, but you lose sight of the overall picture easily, so you should concentrate on concept. You excel in work in which you can deal with the details of an operation and/or numerical perfection.

You are trustworthy in your actions, deliberate in your planning, and firm in your decisions. You are thorough, neat, steady, pragmatic, punctual, patient, and technical.

6 8 5 COMBINATION for: "JANET" or "SCOTT" or equivalent

Your quick thinking gets you out of some close calls. Your creative talents make your job search more flexible and rewarding. Great vision is endowed to those whose names have the mathematical equivalent 685, resulting in business advantages. Great imagination coupled with your ambitious drive brings you closer to your goals at a much quicker speed than your rivals.

Your versatility assures success in every aspect of your business and social life, and your originality and independence secure your future. Your gifted sales abilities make you a leader in the field. Your love of change causes your establishment to lead in sales. The need to communicate is satisfied though social functions and involvement, but you feel a lot more than you express. Sometimes this is a setback if you do not control your impulses and your sensitivity.

You have an inner urge for change and travel that is almost unbearable. You are in constant search of greener pastures. You start many things you have problems finishing; you start with great interest but quickly lose it if the project becomes too monotonous or detailed.

Your desire to understand the forces of nature is awakened early in life. You desire freedom of thought and to think without the interference of others. You would make a great traveling salesperson or aviator. You would also excel in work that allows you freedom of thought and action and work in which you can promote new ideas and/or products.

You are constructive, intuitive, dynamic, and sometimes witty. You must work to control your intolerance, criticism, and impatience.

6 9 6 COMBINATION for: "JENICA" or "MICHAEL" or equivalent

You do not desire to move much in life, and from a young age you love stable and settled conditions. You are a sensible and serious person. Your good judgment, decisiveness, and sense of responsibility would make you a great business executive, but you are versatile in many aspects of your life and can adapt to most conditions. You are gifted with many artistic talents and have an ear for music and the talent to play musical instruments.

You are liked for your tact and diplomacy, and you are able to ease tension among others and prevent many fights. People can come to you to consult about general or personal problems, and they always receive an abundance of useful information. Your intelligence and trustworthiness are highly respected. Your quiet, stable personality is only superseded by your understanding and friendly disposition. You are responsible, honest, and inspirational to others. People can rely on your judgment and depend upon your promises.

You are gifted with the ability to balance the art of living. Nothing can deter you from getting what you want. You have excellent taste and your social activities are numerous; you are more than welcome to attend and lead social activities in your community.

You are studious, mature, and like to do business independently. You are accumulative and responsible for your actions. Your self-confidence brings you success in life as well as an adventurous future. If your name is unbalanced, you will reap some of the negative influences of your first name, which will cause you to worry and try to make others fulfill your desires, as well as to be interfering and intolerant. You must curb the compulsion to care too much for others, as taking on responsibilities for others may be to your detriment.

7 1 8 COMBINATION for: "OLGA" or "JEFFERSON" or equivalent

You could be a great business executive. You are extremely accumulative; your refined nature gets you the better things in life, and your dignified disposition can make you famous. Your sophisticated surroundings result from an appreciation of quality, and your quiet and reserved disposition makes you seem somewhat mystical to others. Your versatility circumvents the most hostile engagement and your talented business sense assures your position. Your mathematical thoroughness raises your success to new heights, particularly in sales.

You are able to organize a business or your private life without training. Your yearning for financial independence is predominant in your life and becomes realized at an early age through your personal independence. Thus, you only accept positions in which you have power and control over commodities and decision-making.

Your ambition seems to allow you to overcome obstacles with ease and your endless energy and stamina help you forge ahead to reach your goals. Your analytical mind quickly assumes responsibility and sometimes you take calculated risks when winning is in your favor. Your solutions are practical and versatile, your powerful nature is accumulative, and your independent character is charitable and honest.

The makeup of your name or its mathematical equivalent allows no transfer of sensitive or general information and suppresses understanding, and the rigid numerical stout-ness in the expression of your name sets a trend of obedi-ence. You have to keep in check your negative emotions, which tend to cause you to over-exaggerate things and make you buy expensive commodities. However, your inner nature is giving; you like to share and help the needy. For this reason, you embrace the universal concepts, organizing and assuming responsibility for others and assisting them in their struggle for justice.

7 2 9 COMBINATION for: "ANGELINA" or "RAYMOND" or equivalent

The above names have no positive qualities to offer, and the remaining negative influences would eventually destroy your divine inner nature. You may become a fanatical religious person with acute perception expressed through undefined hypersensitive emotions.

There is no positive side to the above names and/or mathematical equivalent. If you'd like to make a change to your name please read the information on "Name Analysis" in the last pages of this book.

7 3 1 COMBINATION for: "MONICA" or "RONALD" or equivalent

You express the depth of your feelings and thoughts towards others. Your feelings supersede your actions; you can be blunt when aroused and sarcastic when provoked. You are also quiet and it seems that you go about things deep in thought; you have a natural gift for reflecting on your inner nature and seeking out the mysteries of life. You are a born philosopher and love to dwell in the depths of religion. You can sense a lot more than you may be able to express, causing you to retreat from normal activities while being misunderstood by others. In fact, your sensitivity is acute; you can sense things before they become realized. You can look at people and know what they are going to say before they say it, and this makes others indifferent towards you; they think you are secretive and stuck-up.

You are refined and love the outdoors, finding peace and harmony among the trees, rolling hills, and blue skies. You love to challenge your physical strength with the forces of nature. Little things make you happy; a single flower can arouse deep appreciation while a bouquet of roses would leave you cold.

Your idealistic nature is surpassed by your studious, psychic personality and your natural, gentle ways. You should educate yourself about your emotional shortcomings. In business, your success lies in the practical aspect of things. You are a born leader and you work best in an environment in which your perseverance, self-reliance, and leadership qualities can be introduced.

7 4 2 COMBINATION for: "LYNN" or "MARIO" or equivalent

You are awakened through your desires, but not all of them are realized due to the limited expression capabilities of this name. You are a quiet, reflective, and idealistic person with a great imagination. At times, your thoughts reflect the negative side of your name, and your overly emotional disposition takes control of your mind and body. Your great abilities are dwarfed by your personal depreciation. The positive values of your spirit are imprisoned by misjudgment.

Your lack of self-expression causes you to become withdrawn, and to others you appear cold and aloof. This causes friction for you, as you crave affection and understanding. As a result of your lack of self-confidence, you are unable to cope with the business world. You are a daydreamer, and you like to read fiction. You complain when things go wrong, and your frustration causes or is caused by repression. You withdraw from the world around you.

This name generates the development of physical disorders relating to kidneys, female organs, and fluid functions.

7 5 3 COMBINATION for: "RACHAEL" or "GEORGE" or equivalent

If you have one of the above names and/or the mathematical equivalent 753, as a child you did very well in drama, art, music, speaking, reading, and singing. Early on, you developed a split personality. You appeared to be calm, studious, and refined. Your reflective and inspirational thoughts made you wonder who you were. You are a quiet, determined individual, and you live within your own thoughts. You have a very sensitive religious nature, and you show an interest in religious philosophies and occultism.

Your deep thinking causes you to question everything. You are very secretive, fond of reading and literature, and expressive through the pen. You desire to live and work in an outdoor environment and handle products of the earth. You desire to work independently. You do not have many friends. You can be turbulent and jealous. With inward tension, you lack expression, sociability, and congeniality. All of which can make you become a lone wolf. On the other hand, you have a magnetic and generous nature. Your artistic abilities are accentuated and your happy disposition is reflected in a desire to have the best in life.

Your ambitions have a scientific flavor. You fare well when you can express your creative and artistic abilities. You are a natural entertainer, socially inclined, and a great companion. However, these qualities are sometimes overshadowed by intolerance. You can be argumentative when provoked and impulsive when purchasing. Sometimes you dislike being systematic, come to be untidy, and go overboard in spending.

7 6 4 COMBINATION for: "JOAN" or "HAROLD" or equivalent

System is second nature for you. Your love of study combined with your artistic nature (in "hands-on" categories) brings you personal achievement. If you make good use of your mathematical abilities, you will achieve the ultimate scientific and/or technical life. You are quiet and reserved in your private life. Due to a lack of verbal expression you embrace only a few friends. You must curb your intake of the heavy foods. You are skeptical and demand scientific proof before you accept something as fact. You count the pennies when given change. You have the potential to be a homebody and your cooking is second to none. When others fail while performing monotonous tasks, you are just beginning.

You love tedious projects and your patient and steady efforts always win in the end. Your analytical ability helps you access nature's innermost secrets. You lose sight of the overall picture easily, so you should concentrate on concept. You excel in work in which you can deal with the details of an operation and/or numerical perfection. You have a strong, stable, rugged personality and a steadfast, stable character to match. You are trustworthy in your actions, deliberate in your planning, and firm in your decisions. You are thorough, neat, and steady. You are pragmatic, punctual, patient, and technical.

7 7 5 COMBINATION for: "SOPHIA" or "DONALD" or equivalent

You are quiet and it seems that you go about things deep in thought. You have a natural gift for reflecting on your inner nature and seeking the mysteries of life. You are a born philosopher and love to dwell in the depths of religion. You can sense a lot more than you may be able to express, causing you to retreat from normal activities while being misunderstood by others; you should educate yourself about your emotional shortcomings.

Your idealistic nature is surpassed by your studious, psychic personality and your natural, gentle ways. You love the outdoors, finding peace and harmony among the trees, rolling hills, and blue skies. Your desire to understand the forces of nature is awakened early in life, as well as freedom and the ability to think without the interference of others. You would make a great traveling salesperson or aviator. You would also excel in work that allows you freedom of thought and action and in which you can promote new ideas and/or products.

You are refined, constructive, intuitive, dynamic, and sometimes witty. Little things make you happy; a single flower can arouse deep appreciation while a bouquet of roses would leave you cold. Your inner urge for change and travel is almost unbearable. You are constantly in search of greener pastures. You start many things you have problems finishing; you start with great interest but quickly lose it if the project becomes too monotonous or detailed.

You must work hard to control your impulsive reactions and your sensitive emotions, as well as your intolerance, criticism and impatience.

7 8 6 COMBINATION for: "DELORES" or "HOWARD"or equivalent

The above names and their mathematical equivalent belong to people with a successful business background. Your name is reserved, dignified, and appreciative. You love music, art, and drama. You are very responsible and accumulative, fond of home and quiet surroundings. You cannot easily be understood and have few friends. It is your purpose to take on responsibility for others and your duty to care for the needs of others.

Organization is your defining quality. You are able to organize your business and personal life in your sleep. You are a potential business executive. People can consult with you about general or personal problems; they always receive an abundance of useful information. You are gifted with the ability to balance the art of living.

Your social activities are numerous and you are more than welcome to attend and lead social activities in your community. Your intelligence and trustworthiness are highly respected. Your quiet, stable personality is only superseded by your understanding and friendly disposition. You are responsible, honest, and inspirational to others. You have excellent taste. You are studious, mature, and like to do business independently from others. You are accumulative in your endeavors and responsible for your actions. People can rely on your judgment and depend upon your promises.

7 9 7 COMBINATION for: "VICTORIA" or "PHYL" or equivalent

The above names and/or mathematical equivalent 797 would turn you into an intensely reflective and sensitive person. You get hurt easily and offended by the slightest word against you. You crave affection but seldom find anyone who understands your nature. You can express your thoughts best through the pen. You love the beauty of nature and adore the outdoors. You do not like crowds and you are suspicious of everything. Laughter and light pleasantry are not part of this quality vibration. This vibration is not fortunate and does not bring accumulation or understanding.

Your idealistic nature is surpassed by your studious, psychic personality and your natural, gentle ways. You are refined and love nature, finding peace and harmony among the trees, rolling hills, and blue skies. Little things make you happy; a single flower can arouse deep appreciation while a bouquet of roses would leave you cold.

You are quiet and it seems that you go about things deep in thought. Your purpose is to express the depth of your feelings and thoughts towards others. You have a natural gift for reflecting on your inner nature and seeking the mysteries of life. You are a born philosopher and love to dwell in the depths of religion. Your sensitivity is acute; you can sense things before they happen. You can look at people and know what they are going to say before they say it, and this makes others indifferent towards you; they

194

think you are secretive and stuck up. You can sense a lot more than you may be able to express, causing you to retreat from normal activities while being misunderstood by others. You should educate yourself about your emotional shortcomings.

8 1 9 COMBINATION for: "SUE" or "COOPER" or equivalent

You are extravagant, with expensive tastes; with this name, you developed a desire to have the good things in life, not only for yourself but also for others. You became very capable and generous, and your mind became very clever, and many with this vibration pursue law school and become lawyers.

It is your purpose to inspire others through the knowledge of the universal wisdom and guide them onto the path leading to their spiritual inheritance. Early in life you recognize the need to search for truth and the desire to share this wisdom with the masses. You are an inspirational guide to many and your need to strive for perfection makes you the expert in your field. You leave the audience spellbound when you speak.

You have to fight indulgence in food and other pleasures of the senses. You are a strong lover and have a temper when aroused. You are very emotional and have shattered ideals and loss of affections. Your sales abilities are intensified under this name and you are sold on self. Your already analytical mind is also intensified under this name, causing nervous conditions.

Through your personal evolution you find the purpose in your life and in the lives of others. Your sensitivity demonstrates your compassion for others and your generosity alleviates their suffering. Your deep religious feelings receive clarity through evolution of self. You begin to understand life as you become involved with others. You should educate yourself and enhance your artistic abilities with poetry. Keep in check your acute psychic powers as they easily can cloud your judgment.

This name causes goiter, female troubles, and thyroid problems.

If you'd like to make a change to your name, please read the information on Name Analysis in the last pages of this book.

8 2 1 COMBINATION for: "SUSIE" or "BURNETT" or equivalent

You are a practical person, inventive and creative. You are positive by nature and liked by many. Your desires are primarily for money, which is very hard to come by with the above names or mathematical equivalent. Because of this, you are frustrated, which in turn makes you become dominant and self-centered. You surround yourself with material things. You can be candid with others and shrewd when dealing with money or other tangibles. You lack diplomacy, understanding, and sympathy. You call only a few friends.

Your feelings supersede your actions. You possess strong sexual desires, and you can be blunt when aroused and sarcastic when provoked. In business, your success lies in the practical aspect of things. You are a born leader and you work best in an environment in which your perseverance, self-reliance, and leadership qualities can be introduced.

You love the outdoors and you find peace and tranquility in nature. You love to challenge your physical strength with the forces of nature.

8 3 2 COMBINATION for: "LUCILLE" or "JONATHAN" or equivalent

You are a diplomatic and highly sociable person. You desire the finer things in life and you care for others. You have a pleasant personality. You must curb your desire to take it easy. You desire to become involved in business, organizing and handling finances. With your dependable character and commanding mind you are capable of maintaining control in the business world.

As a child you developed the skill to handle people diplomatically and you could sense the feelings of others. Your favorite subjects were art, fiction, decorating, and music, but you could not be made to hurry in your studies. Undoubtedly you will develop one or more of the negative aspects of this name combination: you may be unscrupulous, unjust with others, materialistic, domineering, calculating, and/or completely self-possessed.

By nature you are a sensitive, refined person who opposes turmoil and hardship of any kind. You like to be involved in the remedying of human suffering, which you cannot bear to witness personally. Witnessing atrocities committed on others causes you tremendous agony. You need to educate yourself to be more active with your mind and body, because, too often, you have the tendency to want to take it easy. Your natural craving for peace and happiness is the source of the slow pace with which you like to set things in motion. Learn to confront adversities and be decisive in your actions. Get involved in decision-making with others through your diplomatic talents. Become in-volved in the problems of others to find success and hap-piness in the wake of your accomplishments. In business, you could do very well working with the public.

8 4 3 COMBINATION for: "LUISE" or "ROMEO" or equivalent

You have an unequaled eye for quality. You have artistic and musical talents and are extremely sociable. You need to curb your spending, which is the result of an urge to dress nicely. You should also refrain from eating too many rich foods and indulging in parties, though your strong sex urges take care of some of the calories.

In business and in your personal life, you love to entertain and express yourself. Selling new, groundbreaking products excites you. You dress immaculately, like to show off on stage, and perform best in large crowds; in fact, you're always performing. Your quick thinking rescues you from imminent disaster. You have an active imagination, which can go overboard. Your devotion to your loved ones is spontaneous and your outlook on life is cosmopolitan. Your adaptability keeps you employed. Your pleasant demeanor can be laced with humor and you thrive upon kindness.

Your name plays a major role in your not having enough money. You can maintain a positive disposition through constructive thought and action, keeping at bay negative beliefs about your personal performance.

8 5 4 COMBINATION for: "JUDIE" or "BURLE" or equivalent

Under the influence of the above names and/or the mathematical equivalent, you are developing into a mathematical genius. You are patient with people, pay attention to details, dwell in facts and figures, and are systematic and practical. You also keep track of every cent. You have a keen sense of quality and you work hard to keep accumulating. Unfortunately, the flip side makes you shrewd, materialistic, mean, and too exact for anyone to stand.

Your analytical ability helps you access nature's innermost secrets, but you lose sight of the overall picture easily, so you should concentrate on concept. You excel in work in which you can deal with the details of an operation and/or numerical perfection. You have a strong, stable, rugged personality and a steadfast, stable character to match. You are trustworthy in your actions, deliberate in your planning, and firm in your decisions. You are thorough, neat, and steady. You are pragmatic, punctual, patient, and technical.

8 6 5 COMBINATION for: "JUNE" or "DUKE" or equivalent

You have great vision and through your independence and foresight you meet people via social channels. You love to mix with people and your excellent disposition makes a good impression on others at first sight. Your mind is analytical, and because of it you would make a great salesperson. Your ambitions are reflected in tangible items.

However, this name combination is very much in misalignment with your inner nature; you express a wealth complex and have expensive tastes. You are headstrong and appear to be a know-it-all. You are critical, and often your ambitions outweigh your abilities. You start many things you have problems finishing; you start with great interest but quickly lose it if the project becomes too monotonous or detailed.

Your desire to understand the forces of nature is awakened early in life. You desire freedom of thought and to think without the interference of others. You would make a great traveling salesperson or aviator. You would also excel in work that allows you freedom of thought and action and in which you can promote new ideas and/or products. You are constructive, intuitive, dynamic, and sometimes witty, but you must work to control your intolerance, criticism, and impatience.

8 7 6 COMBINATION for: "MURIEL" or "RUBEN" or equivalent

You are a clever mathematician, you have great patience in your daily tasks, and you are tentative to details, especially when dealing with money and contracts. Your love for facts and figures exceeds your love for money, and that could be why you accumulate. You are precise and systematic in your work, practical when you make decisions, and you keep track of every cent. You are a hard worker and through a sense of quality have created a comfortable home. You are gifted with the ability to balance the art of living. Nothing can deter you from getting what you want.

Your social activities are numerous and you are more than welcome to attend and lead social activities in your community. Your intelligence and trustworthiness are highly respected. Your quiet, stable personality is only superseded by your understanding and friendly disposition. You are responsible, honest, and inspirational to others. You have excellent taste. You are studious, mature, and like to do business independently from others. You are accumulative in your endeavors and responsible for your actions.

8 8 7 COMBINATION for: "DOLORES" or "RUSSELL" or equivalent

The grouping of letters in this name hinders you from expressing the real you, adversely affecting your life and the sacred spirit crying out to be released from its imprisonment. Generally, this name restricts you from developing your inner potential and, later in life, this name would prevent you from expressing those things closest to your heart.

You will never find happiness with this name, as it stops you from acting in the manner you so desperately desire, causing you instead to undertake things you are basically not designed to do. Your natural gift for helping others is dwarfed by the reserved attitude your name demands, and you find yourself serving others through hospital care, nursing, social functions, and/or the scientific community. Instead of expressing yourself through your active imagination, you are forced into a stoic and mundane environment. Although your natural inspirational qualities lead you into many exciting encounters, the religious and philosophical involvement is too intense; this is also the reason why you are searching for answers in the spiritual realm.

You love to market goods and sell through your expressive, spontaneous, and dramatic disposition, but your name leads you instead into a shrewder business world, which you dislike. Directed by your name, your excellent business judgment is forcing you to be secretive and calculating, and contrary to your inner needs, you are forced into antisocial behavior. You are hard to understand, and so you withdraw and become very lonely.

You love nature and the little things in life, which bring sunshine to your lonely heart. Others think you are absent-minded when in reality you are intensely calculating. The only compatible quality this name has to offer you is creativity, and, because of it, early in life you are able to develop the many creative qualities you have to offer others.

This name is extremely undesirable for you, as it prevents you from expressing the wonderful qualities of your inner self given to you through birth, and it forces you into situations that cause you to develop heart problems.

8 9 8 COMBINATION for: "LUCILLE" or "MONROE" or equivalent

You can control and direct people. You adore quality in everything, and you dress to kill. Your interest is in economics. No one can get the better of you, especially in business. You are out for the big fish and large stakes. You judge others by what they have acquired.

You are able to organize a business or your private life without training. The yearning for financial independence is predominant in your life and becomes realized at an early age through your personal independence. Thus, you only accept positions that give you power and control over commodities and decision-making. Your ambition allows you to overcome obstacles with ease and your endless energy and stamina help you forge ahead to reach your goals. Your analytical mind quickly assumes responsibility and sometimes causes you to take calculated risks when winning is in your favor. Your solutions are practical and versatile, your powerful nature is accumulative, and your independent character is charitable and honest. You have to keep in check your negative emotions, which tend to cause you to over-exaggerate things and make you buy expensive commodities. You also have to curb your eating habits.

Your inner nature is giving; you like to share and help the needy. It is your purpose to embrace the universal concepts, to organize and assume responsibility for others and assist them in their struggle for justice.

9 1 1 COMBINATION for: "SUZANNE" or "NICK" or equivalent

You desire to serve others and your positive nature is at times subdued from the frustration of lack of accomplishment. Your hot temper is expressed with a candid tongue. You feel repressed and at those times you are hard to get along with. You desire to inspire others through the knowledge of the universal wisdom and guide them onto the path leading to their spiritual inheritance. Your advanced inspirational inner nature is a natural endowment you are to share with others. You desire to share this wisdom with the masses. You are an inspirational guide to many and your need to strive for perfection makes you the expert in your field. It is your purpose to find new experiences and introduce new concepts to others. A strong drive leads you to establish your identity through individualism. The interference of others makes you aware of your independent character and the need to be free. You are a practical person, inventive in your ideas, creative with your hands, and original in thought.

You possess strong sexual desires. Your feelings supersede your actions...you can be blunt when aroused and sarcastic when provoked. You love the outdoors and you find peace and tranquility in nature. You love to challenge your physical strength with the forces of nature. In business, your success lies in the practical aspect of things. You are a born leader and you work best in an environment in which your perseverance, self-reliance, and leadership qualities can be introduced.

9 2 2 COMBINATION for: "AUDREY" or "KIRBY" or equivalent

You love to be loved, the main reason for your likable personality and pleasant nature. You can be abstract in conversation, and you dream of a better life. Your sensitivity is stirred frequently and your emotions get in the way of a peaceful association with others. You hate to have to make decisions and concentrate on important matters. You are overly generous and have to bear the consequences. Your soft nature is easily influenced to suit others. You are easygoing and it seems you have no worry in the world. Promises are broken and you hate to confront this. You want to take it easy and it is hard for your body to accept otherwise. Your weakness for sweets is a detriment to your teeth and weight. You underestimate your capabilities, leading you to require assistance from others.

You create an environment of sensitive refinement, expressed in tolerance. You bring tact and diplomacy to others. By nature, you are a sensitive, refined person who opposes turmoil and hardship of any kind. You like to be involved in the remedying of human suffering, which you cannot bear to witness personally. Witnessing atrocities committed upon others causes you tremendous agony.
You need to educate yourself to be more active with your mind and body, because, too often you have the tendency to want to take it easy. Your natural craving for peace and happiness is the source for the slow pace with which you like to set things in motion. Learn to confront adversities

and be decisive in your actions. Get involved in decision-making with others through your diplomatic talents. Become involved in the problems of others to find success and happiness in the wake of your accomplishments. In business, you could do very well working with the public.

9 3 3 COMBINATION for: "SUSANNE" or "RICKY" or equivalent

This name intensifies your already strong musical, artistic, and expressive qualities. You are not self-conscious, you desire to be in good company, and your good nature prevents you from holding grudges. The less positive side of this name combination makes you irresponsible and causes you to spend too much. Your sense of material value is limited, so your spending tends to be unnecessary. Nevertheless, you have a happy-go-lucky nature, though sometimes overly emotional and too giving.

Although you inspire others in many ways, you should target your ambitions towards a more rewarding benefit. You are an inquisitive soul and finding the Divine Wisdom should be of no problem to you. Your sensitive nature gets the better of you, and you can experience detrimental consequences if you don't control your compassion for others. Your high ideals of life are fueled by your inspirational inner nature. Your personal desires, wants, and needs should be balanced towards the wants and needs of others. You have a hard time doing this, but your rewards for this are far greater in perspective to acting to the contrary.

On the other hand, if you don't take heed, you only become unhappy and emotionally unstable. Your love for others is overwhelming, and if you go to the extreme, you can get hurt. It is wise for you to walk the golden path right down the middle to make your life a beautiful experience. Enhance your natural gifts in music, art, and drama. Develop them to greater heights for additional tranquility.

9 4 4 COMBINATION for: "SYBIL" or "MURDOCK" or equivalent

Your experiences mostly dwell in the technical field. Your patience is hard to match; you give extreme attention to all matters. When all have failed to solve a tedious project, you methodically solve it. You have little imagination but given a blueprint to follow, no matter how difficult, you come through. Your greatest upset occurs over ridiculously small matters. You need to think about important things longer than most people, but you come up with acceptable answers. You count the change given to you and you are not afraid to ask for the missing two cents. You never go for big undertakings and given a large project you prefer to tackle only a portion of it.

You have problems explaining complicated issues and do much better explaining through the written word. You are skeptical and demand scientific proof before you accept something as fact. When others fail while performing monotonous tasks, you are just beginning. You love tedious projects and your patient and steady efforts always win in the end. Your analytical ability helps you access nature's innermost secrets. You lose sight of the big picture easily, so you should concentrate on concept. You excel in work in which you can deal with the details of an operation and/or numerical perfection. You are a born engineer.

You have a strong, stable, rugged personality and a steadfast, stable character to match. You have the potential to be a homebody and your cooking is second to none. You are trustworthy in your actions, deliberate in your planning, and firm in your decisions. You are thorough, neat, steady, pragmatic, punctual, patient, and technical. In the end, chances are you get what you want.

9 5 5 COMBINATION for: "TINY" or "JIM" or equivalent

You are a very clever and analytical person. You are not very accumulative because of the numerous changes that have taken place in your life. You experience many depressive moments, which lead to improper thoughts. You are disillusioned about not being able to save, causing snap judgments on your part: you judge people immediately by their appearance.

When aroused your temper becomes uncontrollable. You can also become sarcastic and indifferent. It is your purpose to educate and develop your keen sense of truth and logic. You feel a lot more than you express. Sometimes this is a setback if you do not control your impulsiveness or your hypersensitivity.

Your inner urge for change and travel is almost unbearable. You are constantly in search of greener pastures. You start many things you have problems finishing; you start with great interest but quickly lose it if the project becomes too monotonous or detailed.

Your desire to understand the forces of nature is awakened early in life. You must control your intolerance, criticism, and impatience. You desire freedom of thought and the ability to think without the interference of others. You would make a great traveling salesperson or aviator. You would also excel in work that allows you freedom of thought and action and in which you can promote new ideas and/or products. You are constructive, intuitive, dynamic, and sometimes witty.

9 6 6 COMBINATION for: "PAULINE" or "HUGO" or equivalent

You assume too much responsibility for other people. Your family tends to prefer to serve and uplift others with its generous, idealistic character. People with this name possess great talents and are gifted in art, music, and literature.

You are reliable, intellectual, cheerful, patient, responsible, home loving, modest, thrifty but accumulative, and conscientious. Your greatest worry is that you are not doing enough for others. You desire to direct the efforts of others, particularly in large groups. You have strong opinions, are self-reliant, and you desire a stable, well rounded, and accumulative life.

You desire to settle down and assume business responsibilities, handle commodities, and employ others. You are thrifty. You love home and children and desire to marry early and settle down in order to stabilize your efforts. You are a good manager, a good worker, and a clever, quick thinker. To others you appear generous, expressive, artistic, magnetic, and fueled with great ambition. You enjoy drama, playing stringed instruments, and dancing.

People with this vibration are lovable and make excellent nurses, mothers, and fathers. They are fond of people, particularly children and desire a settled environment that focuses on accumulation and family responsibilities.

9 7 7 COMBINATION for: "INGRID" or "IRVING" or equivalent

Your sensitivity demonstrates your compassion for others and your generosity alleviates their suffering. You do not hold grudges and you are affectionate with the needy. Your deep religious feelings receive clarity through evolution of self. You begin to understand life as you become involved with others. You should educate yourself and enhance your artistic abilities with poetry. Keep in check your acute psychic powers, as they can easily cloud your judgment. You are born philosopher and love to dwell in the depths of religion. Your sensitivity is acute. You can sense things before they happen. This makes others indifferent towards you; they think you are secretive and stuck up. You are quiet and it seems that you go about things deep in thought. You are refined and love the outdoors.

Little things make you happy; a single flower can arouse deep appreciation while a bouquet of roses would leave you cold. You can sense a lot more than you may be able to express, causing you to retreat from normal activities while being misunderstood by others. Your idealistic nature is surpassed by your studious, psychic personality and your natural, gentle ways. You should educate yourself about your emotional shortcomings. You love nature and find peace and harmony among the trees, rolling hills, and blue skies.

9 8 8 COMBINATION for: "PHYLLIS" or "BILL" or equivalent

You are good-natured person with a happy disposition. You are not sociable; you are not willing to begin at the bottom, either. You think the world owes you wealth and a comfortable life. You believe you've got it made. Yet you are withdrawn and live alone. You need help bringing your ideas to fruition. You have an enormous ego and pretend to be successful. Your generosity is designed to impress others and you spend your money foolishly.

You have to keep in check your negative emotions, which tend to over-exaggerate things and make you buy expensive commodities. Your short patience turns people away from you. You dislike hard physical labor. Your analytical mind quickly assumes responsibility and sometimes causes you to take calculated risks when winning is in your favor. Your solutions are practical and versatile. Your sensitivity demonstrates your compassion for others and your generosity alleviates their suffering. You do not hold grudges and you are affectionate with the needy.

9 9 9 COMBINATION for: "LILL" or "DUANE" or equivalent

Your artistic abilities are numerous and appreciated by many. Your dramatic appearances and public speeches are highly inspirational. Your dramatization gives the public a good idea of what to expect from you. Your need to help others is demonstrated in your generosity. Your strong emotional nature is reflected in your intense temper. Your lack of firmness makes your character weak and your personality scattered. Your jealousies trigger self-pity, and with that you lack system and neglect yourself. You love to be waited upon and your interpretation of life is not shared by anyone else.

There are more negative than positive sides to the above names and/or mathematical equivalent. If you'd like to make a change to your name, please read the information on Name Analysis in the last pages of this book.

Conclusion

You are approaching the fork in the road that either sets you free or leaves you in bondage.

With the following pages, I am inviting you to take a very important step in your life.

Educate and inspire yourself to allow your spirit, body, and soul to obtain equilibrium, thus embracing spiritual inheritance. Offer health to your body and happiness to your soul, and achieve success in your endeavors.

Analysis of Life

When you think of mathematics, disregard the old idea that it is a man-made measurement, or a bookkeeping system. Instead, think of this universal principle as the highest form of intelligence, the Spiritual Universal Consciousness. It has dimension whether or not a person measures it. Thus, we see form is dimension and it is both mathematical and spiritual.

Pathway to God

Numerical values are the pathway to God. They contain the spiritual vibration and the physical manifestation in the analysis of life. There are no accidents; all is circumstantial, created by the individual balance of the mind, through a name. Physical and mental disease and the condition of a business are realized through the relationship between a person and nature and through the insight of the natural and mental laws, which govern them. A person operating a business through the Divine Wisdom maintains a powerful tool through which to read the changes, experiences and degrees of success of an individual or business life cycle, and the potential to forecast events and cyclic conditions of nature.

The spirit is eternal,
Your soul longing for a rest.
The ignorance is fraternal,
With just balance surely you will crest.

—Garrett Sinclaire

Services Offered

Business Name Analysis

The returns of a business are only realized if the desires of the business are identical to the vibrations of its birth date, and represent the company in proper perspective. If the company is a registered entity, it is important that the full title of the company be properly displayed at all times. For example, the abbreviation "Co." can cause a severe discord and destroy the corporation; therefore, the desires of the corporation would never be realized.

If the business is a new business, the location, status of the city, county, state, and country may play a major role in the start-up of the business. If the business is an existing organization, a re-birth and relocation may be necessary to succeed.

Big business has the necessary finance to make a success happen, with unavoidable large losses. The small business, with limited capital, cannot afford the luxuries of large losses, and it must succeed to survive. For a small business to become a big conglomerate it may take centuries. However, if the same small business applied the supreme wisdom, with proper management its success would be assured. This small business would have the opportunity to become a large enterprise within nine years, having realized its set goals and satisfied its desires.

If a company desires to operate for a specific period of time, Infinity-Link's method can help it attain success. The application of the Infinity-Link method can assist an existing business in its desire to expand, and insure a turnaround for the business that is failing or cannot get off the ground.

It is the steady progression, hour upon hour, day upon day, that delineates years, centuries, and the greater ages. But, it is the human mind utilizing the passage of years that creates the quality of ages. If a person is to start a project intending to accumulate money, the project must pass through all the different stages or cycles for accumulation to be realized. Just as plants in nature must go through the starting period, growth cycle, and completion period before fruition is possible, a business must also follow the law of relativity. However, the length of a cycle is relative to the size of the project. Whatever unfolds, for good or bad, is the direct result of thought and action. The ability to harness time determines the sum total of life, and in the greater picture, the nature of the ages, for the mind is the only true creative channel on Earth.

Science and business both recognize the existence of rhythmic cycles. The repeating appearances of sunspots, and planetary bodies moving with mathematical regularity, also apply to the rise and fall of markets. There are cycles relative to stock market booms and crashes. Different cycles apply to the economic system, and the average life expectancy of the human specie. A greater year cycle denotes the era of the rise and fall of nations and world powers, and there are cycles that apply to the time when all life on Earth will end.

The Business Name Analysis includes the following:

1. Introduction
2. Birth Date
3. Starting Date
4. Day of Birth
5. Company Name
6. Business Address
7. Telephone Numbers
8. State, County, and City
9. Business Calendar Forecast
10. Important Notices
11. Conclusion

The Business Name Analysis does not include a new balanced business name. This is undertaken separately, and only at the client's request.

Business Calendar Forecast

The Business Calendar Forecast is a precision instrument, which will take the guesswork out of decision-making. It offers guidance through all phases of start-ups and leads a business to the ultimate success with maximum possible profits. It provides yearly and monthly summaries, daily and hourly guidelines on what to do when. Included are action indicators to give your business the necessary advantage against competition and opposition.

Business Start-Up Date

Although there are other important aspects to consider, two particular factors play a paramount role in the success of a business: the start-up date and the name of a business. The start-up date or birth date must be placed into a specific period of time to allow the business to commence, continue and complete the purpose for which it was designed. Once the desired location of a proposed business entity is found, the next step is to find a suitable date for its birth. To receive the correct start-up date, two areas must be considered: first, to set the company in the starting cycle; and second, to receive a path relative to the desires of the business.

The Cyclic Law

Life unfolds through a definite pattern of growth. There is a natural time to start something new, a time to see to details, and a time to reap the rewards for your efforts. The life of a business unfolds in a cyclic pattern, and through the application of the mathematical principle to time, the accurate conditions manifesting in the life of a business can be revealed. There is a cyclic pattern, which unfolds in every life form of life, including the life of a business. It is based upon the natural law of growth relative to time. Just as a seed evolves through the successive stages of growth to reach fruition, through the law of relativity, all life forms must work in harmony with the natural law of growth to reach a successful conclusion.

Besides measuring quantity, mathematics is one of the basic Principles of Life, the fundamental basis of all things in the universe. The cyclic law is the application of mathematics to time. Every life form is set into time and it is governed by it from the first breath of life until death.

There are three basic periods, which make up the Cyclic Law and they are the Starting, the Growth and the Fruition periods.

Starting Period

The starting period is the beginning of the new cycle, a time when every effort should be made to commence anything new, such as a business, or make definite changes necessary for further expansion of an existing business. It is the time for action and it is the time to expand the total energy to start or to excel in a business or personal involvement. It is the period which nature relates to planting a seed. Just as the type, quantity and quality of the seed is important, so is the specific time of planting, as both determine the results of the harvest in the fruition period.

Growth Period

It is a time when your energy and capital should be spent strengthening the business foundation and existing business structure. In private life, it is a time when a person should strengthen existing friendships; revitalize the bond between two people and plan for future goals. This is a time when extra care should be taken in personal safety and health. This is a time to hold back production in business, when it is not prudent to make new friends, start anything new, or accept additional responsibilities that will change the present circumstances. After the natural substance and the foundation of the business pass the crucial test, the business sustains rapid growth and realizes its maximum potential.

Fruition Period

This is the time when the results of previous efforts appear and are realized. It is the fruition period of the life cycle. As with plants in nature, the business reaps the rewards of previous efforts. The rewards are relative to the ideals and accomplishments set forth in the seeding and growth periods. This is the time to reap as you have sown. If the starting period of the company is set into the starting period, the maximum returns of this business entity for a nine-year cycle may be 100% percent. If the starting period of the company is set into the second cycle growth period, the maximum returns of this entity for the nine-year cycle may only be 67% percent. And, if the starting period of the company is set into the third cycle completion period, the maximum returns of this entity for the nine-year cycle may only be 33% percent.

Big Business

Big business has the necessary finance to make a success happen, with unavoidable large losses. The small business, with limited capital, cannot afford the luxuries of large losses and it must succeed to survive. For a small business to become a big conglomerate it may take centuries. However, if the same small business applied the Divine Wisdom, with proper management, its success would be assured. This small business would have the opportunity to become a large enterprise within nine years, having realized its set goals and satisfied its desires.

If a company desires to operate for a specific period of time, the Divine Wisdom can help it attain success. The application of the Divine Wisdom can assist an existing business in its desire to expand and insure a turn-around for the business, which is failing or cannot get off the ground.

Accumulation Realized

It is the steady progression, hour-by-hour, day-by-day, which delineates years, centuries and the greater ages. But, it is the human mind, utilizing the passage of years, which creates the quality of ages. If a person is to start a project intending to accumulate money, the project must pass through all the different stages or cycles for accumulation to be realized. Just as plants in nature must go through the starting period, growth cycle and completion period before fruition is possible, a business must also follow the law of relativity. However, the length of a cycle is relative to the size of the project. Whatever unfolds, for good or bad, is the direct result of thought and action. The ability to harness time determines the sum total of life, and in the greater picture, the nature of the ages, for the mind is the only true creative channel on Earth.

Rhythmic Cycles

Science and business both recognize the existence of rhythmic cycles. The repeating appearances of sunspots and planetary bodies moving with mathematical regularity, also apply to the rise and fall of markets. There are cycles relative to stock market booms and crashes. Different cycles apply to the economic system and the average life expectancy of a human being. A greater year cycle denotes the era of the rise and fall of nations and world powers, and there are cycles that apply to the time when all life on Earth will end.

Personal Name Analysis

Your name is the alphabetic alignment of several letters which identify you.

In the letters of your name are the answers for solving problems of mental discord and unbalance. In the same way that science has been able to measure and correlate mathematical relationships between elements and chemicals into formulas, name analysis measures and reveals the workings and formulas of the human mind. Your name represents a mathematical ordering of the alphabet. This is the key to understanding your mind.

Mathematics is Deeply Imbedded in Language

In addition to the mathematical relationships between the letters in language, letters represent a mathematical position, or speed of vibration. Science not only proves all its discoveries through mathematics, but it is forced to express its findings through the power of language. The gift of language is the single trait that separates us from the animal kingdom, and language is the gateway through which all thoughts and discoveries, whether personal or scientific, must be expressed in order to communicate. Language plays a major role in the great wisdom of the universe, and represents one of the Universal Principles of Life.

233

Name Analysis

You will note the various influences, which affect your pattern of thinking. You will begin to understand the relativity of human behavior, and the profound wisdom contained in our Personal Name Analysis. The analytical method and associated wisdom of name analysis were lost for centuries. For fear that the knowledge would be abused, ancient people took it upon themselves to remove the knowledge...the key, code, and formula from the guidebook of life. A balanced name expresses the spiritual qualities of one's self, and is the source of the reflection of the inner qualities through which a person acts, and communicates in the physical world. Each of your names, and your date of birth, influence your thinking and experiences. Some may be similar in nature, thereby accentuating certain qualities, while others may be opposite, and the reaction is counter-productive.

Today, no one is aware of the importance of the mathematical groupings of letters that form a name, nor is it understood that in due time an unbalanced name can mentally and physically destroy a person. With the help of many people, and through the diligent efforts of myself, we are in a position today to remedy the problem one person at a time.

Birth Date

The analysis of your birth date describes your spiritual qualities: those things you 'desire' through birth. It also identifies your character, personality, occupation, and the type of nature of your inner self: the person you are 'supposed to be' through birth.

First Name

The analysis of your first name reveals how much of your inner self is expressed through your name, and how much it is not, why parts of your inner self are imprisoned, and what you must do to change this situation.

Day of Birth

The analysis of your day of birth identifies the group through which you must fulfill your spiritual duty on Earth, plus a comprehensive account of your past, present, and future lives.

Last Name

The analysis of your last name describes the desires, wants, and needs of your family. It identifies hereditary conditions, and how you can remove mental and physical setbacks.

Combined Names

The analysis of your combined names establishes the total of your anxieties, wants and needs, and is expressed through your first and last names with a total of the positive and negative qualities of your personality, character, and inner nature. Although the full details of your date of birth are outlined after the description of your names, a summary of your inner nature will put the qualities of your names into a relative perspective.

Compatibility Analysis

The compatibility analysis raises your awareness, and proves that a happy relationship is far more than just good looks. With this knowledge you can instantly tell who is or is not compatible with you before meeting. The analysis describes compatible types of people, explains the importance of compatibility in all areas of your life, and the problems affecting you if you are not compatible. In the event a person is married, the analysis establishes your shortcomings, and with a Personal Name Analysis for your spouse, what you both must do to ease your tensions through sacrifice. This can be difficult to do, but perhaps better than a total separation.

How do you choose a partner? Do you choose by looks, first impression, or what a friend told you? Looks are only skin-deep. Impressions don't last. A friend's opinion is based on that person's observation. When you go by looks, you only get what you see! If you go by first impression, you don't receive depth! If you go by what a friend tells you, you'd better stay single!

Wherever you go, whatever you do, you are constantly confronted with the sometimes frightening thought: "*How will I make out?*"

Simply because we don't know the person we are going to meet we have to put on our best behavior—best clothes and false charm just to please others. Most of the time this is ignored, at best. The only time we can be ourselves is when we are alone.

With a Compatibility Analysis, you have the chance to re-alize your wants, needs and desires, and live them to the fullest with a partner who is 100% compatible with you. You both can share the entire spectrum of your character, personality, and inner natures, enjoying them in unison. All this starts to happen by doing the first things first: hav-ing your name analyzed.

Mini Name Analysis™

A Mini Name Analysis™ analyzes your birth date and your first name. The Mini Name Analysis™ is the introduction to the 40-page Personal Name Analysis. The Mini Name Analysis™ identifies your inner self, the person you are within. It reveals you inner desires and describes your character, personality, and vocation.

Your first name analysis tells you who you are now through your first name states the degree of compatibility between your inner nature and your first name. The Mini Name Analysis™ also describes what you must do if your first name and inner nature are not compatible in order to live a healthy and successful life.

The Mini Name Analysis™ will give you a good understanding of the accuracy of this powerful knowledge. You will note the various influences affecting your pattern of thinking, and you will find the information exciting and unusual. In order to comprehend the complete concept, we urge you to read the entire document at least twice. You will begin to understand the relativity of human behavior and the information contained in this analysis.

A name expresses the spiritual qualities of the self, and is the source of the reflection of the inner qualities through which a person acts and communicates in the physical world. Each of your names, and your date of birth, influence your thinking and experiences. Some may be similar in nature, thereby accentuating certain qualities, while others may be opposite, and the reaction is counter-productive.

The knowledge and associated wisdom to obtain a balanced name was lost for centuries through the theft of a group of people who feared that the knowledge would be abused.

They took it upon themselves to remove the knowledge...the key, code, and formula from the guidebook of life. Today, no one is aware of the importance of the mathematical groupings of letters that form a name, nor is it understood that in due time an unbalanced name can mentally, and physically destroy a person. With the help of many people, and through the diligent efforts of myself, we are in a position today to remedy the problem one person at a time.

Personal Calendar Forecast

Language is the gateway through which all thoughts and discoveries, whether personal or scientific, must be expressed in order to communicate. Language plays a major role in the universe and represents one of the Universal Principles of Life.

We are born into time. The date of our birth determines both the spiritual potential we are born to fulfill and our personal cyclic position relative to the universe. If we are unaware of our role, we will not find peace, happiness, contentment or success. Instead, we will be like a ship without a rudder, hoping for the best but almost always attracting the worst. We cannot go against the basic law of cycles and find prosperity. Our Personal Calendar Forecast is based on the Universal Cyclic Law. Our yearly Personal Calendar Forecast consists of a detailed summary explaining highlights of the present year cycle, including twelve monthly summaries outlining long-range forecasts, itemized for each day with hourly guidelines and action indicators.

The Cyclic Law

Life unfolds through a definite pattern of growth. There is a natural time to start something new, a time to see to details and a time to reap the rewards for your efforts. The life of a business unfolds in a cyclic pattern, and through the application of the mathematical principle to time, the accurate conditions manifesting in the life of a business can be revealed. There is a cyclic pattern, which unfolds in every life form, including the life of a business. The cyclic pattern is based upon the natural law of growth relative to time. Just as a seed evolves through the successive stages of growth to reach fruition, through the law of relativity, all life forms must work in harmony with the natural law of growth to reach a successful conclusion. Besides measuring quantity, mathematics is one of the basic Principles of Life; the fundamental basis of all things in the universe. The cyclic law is the application of mathematics to time. Every life form is set into time at birth and governed by it from the first breath of life until death.

Nothing happens by chance; there is a logical cause or reason for every effect.

There are three basic periods that make up the Cyclic Law, and they are the Starting, the Growth and the Fruition periods.

Starting Period

The starting period is the beginning of the new cycle. A time when every effort should be made to commence anything new, such as a business, or make definite changes necessary for further expansion of an existing business. It is the time for action and it is the time to expand the total energy to start or to excel in a business or personal involvement. It is the period which nature relates to planting a seed. Just as the type, quantity and quality of the seed is important, so is the specific time of planting, as both determine the results of the harvest in the fruition period.

Growth Period

This is a time when your energy and capital should be spent strengthening the business foundation and existing business structure. In private life, it is a time when a person should strengthen existing friendships; revitalize the bond between two people and plan for future goals. This is a time when extra care should be taken in personal safety and health. This is a time to hold back production in business, when it is not prudent to make new friends, start anything new, or accept additional responsibilities that will change the present circumstances. After the natural substance and the foundation of the business pass the crucial test, the business sustains rapid growth and realizes its maximum potential.

Fruition Period

This is the time when the results of previous efforts appear and are realized. It is the fruition period of the life cycle. As with plants in nature, the business reaps the rewards of previous efforts. The rewards are relative to the ideals and accomplishments set forth in the seeding and growth periods. This is the time to reap as you have sown.

If the starting period of the company is set into the starting period, the maximum returns of this business entity for a nine-year cycle may be 100% percent. If the starting period of the company is set into the second cycle growth period, the maximum returns of this entity for the nine-year cycle may only be 67% percent. And, if the starting period of the company is set into the third cycle completion period, the maximum returns of this entity for the nine-year cycle may only be 33% percent.

———————

Index

A

B

M

N

S

Infinity-Link Publishing
1517 N. Wilmot PMB 134
Tucson, AZ. 85712
Phone: 520-298-7391 - Fax: 425-920-7687
www.itsinyourname.com

PRODUCT LIST

(A) *It's In Your Name* by Garrett Sinclaire
5½ x 8½ hardcover
US $26
(B) The Name Game CD - Complete formula to analyze any first name US $17
(C) First Name Analysis US $12

Infinity-Link Personal and Business Name Analyses

(1) Personal Name Analysis (45 Pages) US $250
(2) Rush Orders US $260
(3) Business Name Analysis (50 Pages) US $450
(4) Rush Orders US $480

Infinity-Link Personal Compatibility Analysis

(5) Personal Compatibility Analysis for Two Individuals
(20 Pages) US $40
(5A) Mini Compatibility Analysis for Two Individuals US $20

Infinity-Link Personal and Business Calendar Forecasts

(6) Yearly Personal Calendar Forecast (120 Pages) US $120
(7) Quarterly Personal Calendar Forecast (40 Pages) US $40
(8) Yearly Business Calendar Forecast (120 Pages) US $150

(9) Quarterly Business Calendar Forecast (40 Pages) US $50
(10) Personal Mini Name Analysis for Two Individuals US $25
   Add $5.00 per month for rush orders
  Prices are subject to change without notice

Allow 1 Week Delivery

Order number(s) from Product Price List: (__), (__), (__), (__),
(__), (__), (__), (__), (__), (__), (__), (__)

Subtotal: $_____Plus S&H $_____

Total Charge: $_____

Signature:_____

Date:_____

Please add Shipping and Handling
Mini Analysis US $2.00 per order.
All other orders US $5.00 per order.
Standard Orders Allow 3 Weeks Delivery -
Rush Orders Allow 1 Week Delivery
- Prices are subject to change without notice -
Send information together with your check or money order
payable to Infinity-Link to the address above.

For online and credit card orders go to:
www.itsinyourname.com/o2_products-services.htm

Infinity-Link Publishing
1517 N. Wilmot PMB 134
Tucson, AZ. 85712
Phone: 520-298-7391 - Fax: 425-920-7687
www.itsinyourname.com

PERSONAL AND BUSINESS
NAME ANALYSIS

ORDER FORM

Please print clearly and spell information accurately.

Date:_____ Telephone: _____

Address:_____

City:_____

State/Province:_____Zip/Postal Code:_____

E-Mail:_____

Fax:_____

Birth Date:_____

Current last name and years used:

_____

Registered first name:

_____

Registered last name:

_____

If married, state maiden name and years used:

_____

Nicknames, years used:

_____

Signature:
_____

Print Signature:
_____

BUSINESS NAME ANALYSIS
supply additional information below

Company Name:_____

Date registered: _____

Corporation:____ or Doing Business As: ____

City of registration: _____

County of registration:_____

State of registration: _____

Personal Name Analysis (45 Pages)US $250
Rush Orders US $260
Business Name Analysis (50 Pages) US $450
Rush Orders US $480
Shipping and Handling: Add US $4.50
Standard Orders Allow 3 Weeks Delivery - Rush Orders Allow 1-Week Delivery
- Prices are subject to change without notice -
Send information together with your check or money order payable to Infinity-Link to the address above.

For online and credit card orders go to:
www.itsinyourname.com/o2_products-services.htm

Infinity-Link Publishing
1517 N. Wilmot PMB 134
Tucson, AZ. 85712
Phone: 520-298-7391 - Fax: 425-920-7687
www.itsinyourname.com

PERSONAL OR BUSINESS
CALENDAR FORECAST
ORDER FORM
Please print clearly and spell information accurately.

Personal _____ Business_____

Date: _____

Home Telephone: _____ Office Telephone: _____

Address: _____

City: _____

State/Province: _____ Zip/Postal Code: _____

E-Mail: _____

Fax: _____

First Name: _____

Last Name: _____

Quarterly Forecast beginning month: _____

Yearly Forecast for year: _____

Signature:

FOR BUSINESS CALENDAR FORECAST ADD:

Company Name:_____

Yearly Personal Calendar Forecast (120 Pages)   US $120
Quarterly Personal Calendar Forecast (40 Pages)   US $40
Yearly Business Calendar Forecast (120 Pages)   US $150
Quarterly Business Calendar Forecast (40 Pages)   US $50

Add $5.00 per month for rush orders.
Shipping and Handling: Add US $7.50
Standard Orders Allow 3 Weeks Delivery - Rush Orders Allow 1
Week Delivery
- Prices are subject to change without notice -
Send information together with your check or money order
payable to Infinity-Link to the address above.

For Online and Credit Card orders go to:
http://www.itsinyourname.com/o2_products-services.htm -

Infinity-Link Publishing
1517 N. Wilmot PMB 134
Tucson, AZ. 85712
Phone: 520-298-7391 - Fax: 425-920-7687
www.itsinyourname.com

PERSONAL COMPATIBILITY ANALYSIS
ORDER FORM

Please print clearly and spell information accurately.

Date: _____ Telephone: _____

Address: _____

City: _____

State/Province: _____ Zip/Postal Code: _____

E-Mail: _____

Fax: _____

First Party to be analyzed:

Birth Date: _____

First Name:
_____

Last Name:
_____

Current Last Name:
_____

If married, state maiden name and years used:
_____

Nicknames, state years used:
_____

Signature:

Print Signature:

Second Party to be analyzed:

Birth Date:_____

First Name:

Last Name:

Current Last Name:

Nicknames, state years used:

Signature:

Print Signature:

Personal Compatibility Analysis for two individuals (20 Pages)
US $40.00
Shipping and Handling: Add US $5.00
Please Allow 3 Weeks for Delivery
- Prices are subject to change without notice -
Send information together with your check or money order
payable to Infinity-Link to the address above.

Online and Credit Card orders go to:
http://www.itsinyourname.com/o2_products-services.htm

Infinity-Link Publishing
1517 N. Wilmot PMB 134
Tucson, AZ. 85712
Phone: 520-298-7391 - Fax: 425-920-7687
www.itsinyourname.com

MINI-COMPATIBILITY ANALYSIS
ORDER FORM

Please print clearly and spell information accurately.

Date:_____ Telephone: _____

Address:_____

City:_____

State/Province:_____ Zip/Postal Code:_____

E-Mail:_____

Fax:_____

First Party to be analyzed:

Birth Date:_____

First Name:
_____

Last Name:
_____

Current Last Name:
_____

If married, state maiden name and years used:
_____

Nicknames, state years used:
_____

Signature:

Print Signature:

Second Party to be analyzed:

Birth Date: _____

First Name:

Last Name:

Current Last Name:

Nicknames, state years used:

Signature:

Print Signature:

Mini Compatibility Analysis for two individuals US $20.00
Shipping and Handling: Add US $2.00
Please Allow 3 Weeks for Delivery
- Prices are subject to change without notice -
Send information together with your check or money order
payable to Infinity-Link to the address above.

Online and Credit Card orders:
http://itsinyourname.com/o2_products-services.htm

Infinity-Link Publishing
1517 N. Wilmot PMB 134
Tucson, AZ. 85712
Phone: 520-298-7391 - Fax: 425-920-7687
www.itsinyourname.com

PERSONAL MINI-NAME ANALYSIS
ORDER FORM

Please print clearly and spell information accurately.

Date: _____ Telephone: _____

Address: _____

City: _____

State/Province: _____ Zip/Postal Code: _____

E-Mail: _____

Fax: _____

Birth Date: _____

Current last name and years used:

_____

Registered first name:

_____

Registered last name:

_____

If married, state maiden name and years used:

_____

Nicknames, years used:

_____

Signature:

Print Signature:

Personal Mini-Name Analysis for two individuals US $25.00
Shipping and Handling: Add US $2.00
Please Allow 3 Weeks for Delivery
- Prices are subject to change without notice -
Send information together with your check or money order
payable to Infinity-Link to the address above.

Online and Credit Card orders:
http://www.itsinyourname.com/o2_products-services.htm

Infinity-Link Publishing
1517 N. Wilmot PMB 134
Tucson, AZ. 85712
Phone: 520-298-7391 - Fax: 425-920-7687
www.itsinyourname.com

FIRST NAME ANALYSIS
ORDER FORM

Please print clearly and spell information accurately.

Date:_____

Hard Copy Analysis_____ The Name Game CD Purchase_____

Shipping Address:_____

First Name:_____

Last Name:_____

Address: _____

City: _____

State/Province: _____ Zip/Postal Code: _____

E-Mail: _____

Fax: _____

Registered First Name to be analyzed:_____

Contact:_____

Telephone: _____

E-Mail address: _____

Signature:

_____

Print Signature:

_____

First Name Analysis US $12.00   - The Name Game CD US
$17.00
Shipping and Handling: Add US $2.00
Please Allow 3 Weeks for Delivery
- Prices are subject to change without notice -
Send information together with your check or money order
payable to Infinity-Link to the address above.

Online and Credit Card orders:
http://www.itsinyourname.com/o2_products-services.htm

The Name Game CD

contains a unique secret, ancient formula

Infinity-Link's "THE NAME GAME" CD Purchase

Discount Coupon

Send this discount coupon together with the original pay receipt

of this book and The Name Game order Form to:

Infinity-Link, PMB #134 -1517 N. Wilmot, Tucson, Arizona 85712, U.S.A.

To receive a 20% discount on the posted purchase price

of Infinity-Link's "THE NAME GAME" CD.

Infinity-Link

James Mathew

Copyright (c) 2001, Garret Sinclaire

Enter the letters of any first name, select the submit button
and discover the exciting and fascinating qualities of that
name from the detailed read-out.

It's In Your Name CD

**contains a complete copy of the unabridged
electronically formatted version of the book
It's In Your Name.**

Infinity-Link's "It's In Your Name" CD Purchase

Discount Coupon

Send this discount coupon together with the original pay receipt

of this book and It's In Your Name order Form to:

Infinity-Link, PMB #134 –1517 N. Wilmot, Tucson, Arizona 85712, U.S.A.

To receive a 20% discount on the posted purchase price

of Infinity-Link's It's In Your Name CD.

Infinity-Link

James Mathew

Copyright (c) 2001, Garred Sinclaire